No Money Down Property Investing

Kevin McDonnell

No Money Down Property Investing by Kevin McDonnell
www.nomoneydownbook.co.uk

Design by Thom Luter & Luke Bunting
Research by Kevin McDonnell
© Copyright 2018 Kevin McDonnell

Note for Librarians: A cataloguing record for this book is available from Library and Archives Canada at www.collectionscanada.gc.ca/a-z-index/index-e.html

Printed in Peterborough, Cambridgeshire, UK ISBN: 978-1-909846-76-0

Published by Progressive Publishing
Progressive House
Units 8, 9, 10
Cygnet Park, Forder Way, Hampton Peterborough, PE7 8GX

Facebook: www.facebook.com/kevinMcDonnell3
Twitter: twitter.com/KevinMc_Donnell
Instagram: Instagram.com/kevinmcdonnell77
www.kevinmcdonnell.co.uk

About Kevin McDonnell

Kevin McDonnell is regarded as the foremost expert in the UK when it comes to creative property investment strategies.

If you met him today he would tell you that he was probably one of the worst property investors in the world when he initially started out on his property investment journey, and that he made every mistake imaginable in the first few years, resulting in him finding himself over £135,000 in debt.

The only thing he did right in his first 10 years in property was that he kept going, and realising he needed to get educated, he researched, followed and learnt from every successful property investor he could find.

Kevin is now a multiple business owner and has become a self-made millionaire thanks to property, building a multi-million-pound portfolio using creative No Money Down property investment techniques.

As well as continuing to build his property businesses, he now teaches others how they too can build a successful property portfolio starting with little or no money. If Kevin can do it, so can you.

Acknowledgements

I would like to take this opportunity to thank everyone who has been a part of my journey to date – not just in property, but also in life. Without realising it, you have all supported me in some way, either directly or indirectly, on my journey and helped me get to the point where I am in a position to be able to share the No Money Down property investment strategies with the world.

Being Irish, I could probably list two pages of names before I've even finished listing family, so I'm not going to make an enormous list of everyone who has impacted my life. But if you were a part of my journey in childhood or in my previous working life, if you were a colleague, mentor, mentee, student or friend, I have learnt a phenomenal amount from you all, and I wouldn't be the person I am or where I am today without you.

All that being said, there are some people I must highlight for special acknowledgement for the contributions and support you have given me – without you, my lifestyle and this book would not have been possible. Thank you to Rob Moore, Mark Homer, Paul O'Mahoney, Tony Robbins,

Ray O'Rourke, Des O'Rourke, Kevin Green, Gill Fielding, Dr John Demartini, Jim Rohn, Brian Tracey, Mark Dalton, Richard Branson, Sanjiv Sethi, Robert Kiyosaki, Daniel Wagner, Grant Cardone, all my mentees & mentors on the No Money Down Mastermind and all the speakers, trainers and staff at Progressive Property.

I would also like to thank all my staff who have helped me grow and freed me from working in my business so that I could get this book out there.

Finally, I would like to thank my late father, my mum, brother and sisters for everything you have done for me in life, but especially my wife Linda for supporting me unreservedly on my journey over the last five years. I was living in a room in a shared house when we met, and you and our beautiful son Rikardo have given me the inspiration and drive to change my life in ways I never thought imaginable. I have spent 12 days away from you both writing this book, and they have been the most difficult and yet rewarding 12 days of my life. Thank you for all your patience and understanding, I love you!

Contents

Chapter 1: Introduction

How many houses would you have if you could get them for free? What if I was to tell you that you can? I have used No Money Down Property Investment techniques to build a multi-million-pound property portfolio, and in this book I will share with you exactly how I did it – and how you can too.

I have thought about writing a book for a long time and kept putting it off, but finally I managed to get it done. I am not a professional writer, I'm just somebody with an interest in property and a burning desire to be successful and help others in any way I can. I have read a lot of property books, and they have generally all been about how to buy property. Often the strategies taught were great, but they required money for implementation. I don't know about you, but the one thing I didn't have when I started out was money; the whole point of getting into property was to create the money.

The one thing that always seems to be missing for me in the books I read is how I could not only get started, but also build a large, scalable property business using none of my own money. This book is full of detailed descriptions of the various No Money Down Investment techniques that I, and hundreds of other people I have taught, use to build massive cash flow from property. They include strategies that require no money, very little money, none of your own money and no money left in.

I wanted to open people's minds to the various creative strategies that you can use today to start or scale your property business. The other key focus throughout this book is highlighting the potential pitfalls of each strategy. That's not to put you off investing but rather to ensure you are aware of the risks, so that you mitigate them and to not make the same poor newbie decisions I made when I was starting out. The smart thing to do is to learn from someone else's mistakes and not from your own. I have walked the road before you and made the mistakes; you don't have to if you learn from mine. I'm not saying you will never make a mistake, but what you can do is make your mistakes small. The only people who have never made a mistake are people who have never done anything. If you want to be successful, then mistakes are part of the journey; however, you can reduce the likelihood of making mistakes by learning from others and increasing your knowledge.

I firmly believe that property is one of the most forgiving businesses in the world. I use the word business and not investment because if you are to be successful, then you need to treat it as a business, and not just an investment, from day one. There are several reasons why property is forgiving, which I will touch on throughout the book, but some of the key reasons are:

1. If you keep the property let to tenants and the rent covers the mortgage, then you can keep for the long term, even if it's in negative equity.

2. If anything goes wrong or you buy a bad property, you can use different strategies such as 'options' to make money from the deal.

3. History has taught us that over the long term, property prices will rise, so if you can afford to hold long term, you will make a profit.

4. Inflation kills the debt – more on this later.

Often when I speak to people who are in property, or thinking about getting into property, they say they want to 'own' property. However, when I dig a little deeper, they realise that they don't actually want to own property. It's not the bricks and mortar that people want, it's the cash flow the property creates that they're really after.

Why not just focus on the CASHFLOW? This is because most people believe that you need to own property to create the cash. However, the richest people on the planet live by different principles – over one hundred years ago, John D Rockefeller said: "Own Nothing but control everything."

Some of the strategies in this book will show you how you can 'buy' property to leave a long-term legacy, and other strategies will focus on how to 'control' property to create massive cash flow to get you the time and freedom to build a large, scalable business.

How I started

I received an email from an American company inviting me to a free three-hour workshop, claiming they could teach people how to buy property professionally. I didn't have a clue what 'professionally' meant and was very cynical about their claims. However, I decided to attend anyway, more to prove to myself that you didn't need to be taught how to buy a house. After all, I'm Irish – we build our own houses and that's a lot more difficult that handing over some money for one!

I sat through the three hours listening to this American guy telling everyone about all these different ways to buy property, and it really resonated with me. I thought to myself, *this is what I want to do with my life, I want to be a property investor*. At the end of the session I was offered a training course for £1,800, which would teach me everything I needed to know to get started in property. I remember telling myself that this was a waste of money and I could do it myself; I mean, how difficult could it be, right? Hindsight really is a wonderful thing. Had I known then what I know now, that would have been the best £1,800 I would ever have spent. Not paying it cost me well over 6 figures in mistakes.

You see, instead of investing in the training, I went back home and started to research buying property in the UK. I decided that buying in London was too expensive and I would never be able to save a deposit; had I done the training course, I would have learnt lots of ways to make income from property without the need for a deposit. I didn't have much experience, and being new to the country, I didn't know any areas of the UK in detail, so I decided I would ask my uncle who lived near Manchester to help me buy a house. Asking family for help without them understanding investment property either is not a bright idea. I will never forget the day in mid-2003 when I went viewing houses with my aunt and uncle. We had agreed that I needed a nice family home that needed no maintenance and that it would be a bad idea to buy the cheaper houses, as they would require more maintenance. So we naively ended up making an asking price offer on a 3-bed semi-detached house for £82k. Now that's not expensive in today's terms, and even if the deal had gone through (more on that later) I would still have made some profit long-term and probably prevented some of my major mistakes that were to follow. However, we weren't professionally trained – had we been, we would have known this was not the type of property to buy and that houses were available in the real 'goldmine areas' around Manchester for £20-30k back in 2003 that could have been refurbished to add value and create immediate profit. The offer was accepted, and the gents informed us that the couple selling were in a chain and needed to find a house before they could sell (my first experience of a chain was not to be a good one). After three months, and paying out on surveys and solicitors' fees, the deal fell through due to the vendors not finding a suitable property to purchase. I felt terrible; I had spent just over £600 and had nothing to show for it. Unfortunately, it put me off buying property in the UK, and even more unfortunately, it set me on the path to my biggest mistakes... Investing abroad!

It was December 2003 and I had returned home to Ireland to spend Christmas and New Year with my family. Around the same time, lots of overseas property sales companies were springing up, and there were constant advertisements on the radio promoting them. Everyone was talking property and the real buzz was around investing abroad.

Another lesson was about to be learnt: never base an investment decision on a chat in the pub with your mates – they either know less than you or talk about it but don't actually do it.

I, on the other hand was a READY-FIRE-AIM type of guy! So before heading back to London, I popped into a local overseas property sales company.

They gave me the big sales pitch on how great an investment it would be to buy a 1-bedroom apartment in Turkey – there would be guaranteed rent for five years (it's funny how that guaranteed rent doesn't always come about once the apartment is built). I walked out of the shop about an hour later as the owner of a brand new 1-bedroom apartment on the other side of Europe, in a town I had never heard of, with no idea about the local tax laws (or any other laws, for that matter).

Back in the UK, naively believing that I had made a smart investment that was going to make me a small fortune and thinking how easy the whole process was, I set about looking for more 'great investments' overseas...

The perfect 2-bed apartment in Parnu, Estonia

So, with things seemly going well with my Turkish investment, I took a trip to Estonia in September 2005 to view a piece of land that a UK company was going to build a block of apartments on. I was shown lovely brochures and plans for the apartments, and I was taken to the site and shown the views from where my 2-bed apartment would be built. It all seemed great – and a 'steal' at £36k, with an upfront deposit of £9K and the remainder payable on completion of the build.

The problem was I wasn't getting a property for a 'steal', but rather I was being stolen from. Things seemed to start well – when I got back to the UK, I received positive updates on the build for a few months, but then things went quiet. Months and months passed by and no progress; every time I rang the office of the UK investment company they would give me various excuses about problems with builders, until one day when I rang and there was no answer. I did some investigating and it turned out the company had closed down and run off with all the investors' money. On further investigation, the land I was shown during my trip to Estonia never even had planning permission – there were no issues with the builder, there was no building!

Bulgaria

Having returned to the UK after my viewing trip to Estonia, and getting updates on the build, I started to believe that property investing was easy and that everything was going great. So when things are going great, what do you do? ... You do it AGAIN! So I did: in mid-2005, while I was still getting positive updates on the build in Estonia, oblivious to the issues that lay ahead, I decided that I needed to make hay while the sun shines, so I researched online and decided that the next big thing would be Bulgaria. Now, this was my third investment overseas– I had invested in a beach apartment in Turkey and an apartment overlooking a lake in Estonia – so I decided the obvious thing to do now would be a ski apartment in Bansko, Bulgaria. At this stage in my investment journey I felt unstoppable, so I invested in a 2-bed top-floor penthouse apartment for £79,999.

These are some pictures of the Bansko apartment I took when I went to stay there:

I was no longer just any old property investor, I was now an international property investor, or so I thought. The reality was that I was probably the worst property investor in the world. Anyone can buy a house, but a house is not a deal. If any house was a deal, you could just go on Rightmove right now and pick the first one you saw. I quickly realised that I didn't have a clue what I was doing.

Once the development in Bulgaria was finished, I got hit with extortionate management fees. The only person ever to stay in my apartment was me, and when I did they tried to charge me over €200 to stay in my own apartment for just one week. There were 64 apartments (eight blocks of eight apartments in one complex), all owned by English and Irish investors. Under Bulgarian law, you can hold an Extraordinary General Meeting (EGM) and vote out your management company, so that's what we did. Then we voted in a different property management company run by an English couple local to Bansko.

All seemed great initially, but then within weeks of voting in the new management company, the old management company came back to the apartments and stripped them of everything of value; the most shocking thing was that they did this with the help of the local police. They took literally everything of value, even the skylights. A property in a ski resort with no skylights is not a good idea.

A few the owners went over to Bansko and we took the management company to court. We got in front of a judge who asked for proof that the contents belonged to us, as Mr Kalin, head of the local Mafia, had receipts for the purchase of all the contents, and because we voted him out he was just taking back what was his. This was the point at which we realised the property we owned was built by the local Bulgarian Mafia – the whole system was corrupt. The buildings insurance didn't even pay out, as the court confirmed that the contents were not ours! I've never seen a kitchen, air con units and skylights classed as contents before.

I still to this day pay local taxes and insurance on the building, yet it is completely valueless. Yes, I could have refurbished it, but it would still be next door to 63 other completely trashed apartments, and there was always the risk that the Mafia would come back and rip everything out again.

The apartment after it got ripped out.

I thought I was an international property investor with holiday homes across Europe, but the reality was that 18 months after walking away from that £1,800 training course, I had lost £135,000 I didn't have, as they were bought off-plan. I had to take out seven different credit cards and three personal loans to cover the payments of the debt, and it took me 10 years to dig myself out of that hole. That's why I always say if you think education is expensive, you should try ignorance.

I had learnt so much, but it had cost me a fortune and I saw no way out of the mess. It was a really difficult time and I didn't know what to do; I felt so ashamed and embarrassed that I wouldn't go to my family for help. You don't need to make the mistakes I made – I was completely broke, financially and as a person.

I faced a crossroads and had two choices:

- Walk away from all my debt and go bankrupt

- Get myself educated and dig myself out of this mess

After a few years of self-pity and hard work trying to earn my way out of debt in a job, I finally made the decision to face up to my mistakes and I chose to get educated. I read books, I attended training courses and I aligned myself to successful property investors who had achieved what I was trying to. Over the last five years, I have built a multi-million pound property portfolio and several businesses – all with none of my own money. In this book, I will share the very strategies I used, so you can too.

"Life is 10% what happens to me and 90% how I react to it."
– Charles R Swindoll

Why No Money Down Investing?

In my first 10 years in property, I made every mistake you could possibly make and ended up more in debt than when I started. People always ask me what made me keep going and how I learnt to invest using the strategies I teach today. You could say I got lucky, but not luck in the way most people see luck (more on that soon). You see, I had tried for 10 years to save up enough money to buy property the conventional way with deposits, but property prices kept rising at a faster rate than I could save. However, even if I could have saved up enough money, it would still only have been enough for one house; there was no way I could have saved enough to buy 10, 15, 20 properties.

The biggest challenge for most people getting started in property is financing the first deals. Let's be honest: money is the reason we want to get into property, and money is also the reason most people never get started. The reason they don't start in the first place is because they think they need savings to get started. However, this is just not true. The one thing that is true is that you don't know what you don't know!

Now, I know some of you reading this will be very sceptical, thinking NO MONEY DOWN? HOUSES FOR FREE?? YA RIGHT! But please keep reading with an open mind, because that is exactly what I will show you in this book.

The reality is that the only way you can build a large, scalable property business is using No Money Down Investing techniques. I looked at all the very successful property investors – and when I say very successful I mean those who have built portfolios of 50, 60, 100, 200, 500 properties – and I thought, *how could they do this by saving up deposits?* And the thing is, they didn't – they used No Money Down Investing techniques to do it.

This is where I started to get lucky. I still speak to people today (and there will probably be some people reading this book who think the same) who say "he got lucky", "he started at the right time", "you can't do that now", etc. Well, as Henry Ford famously said, "whether you think you can, or you think you can't – you're right." The truth is I didn't get lucky, but I did implement **LUCK** – **L**abour **U**nder the **C**orrect **K**nowledge. I got EDUCATED. I aligned myself to people who were massively successful, and I followed what they were doing. I didn't create any of the strategies you will hear about in this book, I just learnt them and then implemented them – and you can too.

I know that 95% of people reading this book right now will run out of money before they've got five houses. If you are using your own money, you will run out before you've got five deposits for five houses. There are also many property investors who will see this book and think it's not for them – they'll think, *I've got some money, I don't need No Money Down* – but this is not about having money or not having money. This is about not spending your own money! This is about No Money Down Investing. If you have some money, the smart thing to do is leave it in the bank. Invest in yourself, invest a little bit into property. Do not put all your life savings into property – that wouldn't be a smart thing to do, because then the money's tied up and you can't live the life you want to live. Does that make sense? The smart thing to do is to use other people's money. I don't just mean joint venturing with property investors; that is one of the No Money Down strategies I'll detail later in the book, but there are lots of other strategies I'll share too.

Why is knowing these strategies important? I did some research and the results show that knowing these strategies is not just important for you, but critical to your success. My research revealed that the average price of a house in the UK in July 2018 was £223,257, and it's rising all the time. What that means is you would need a £55,814 deposit for just one property (25% deposit based on a 75% loan to value mortgage). That means that some people will have run out of money before they've bought one house, and most people will have run out of money before they've bought five houses. If you're in that position right now, No Money Down Investing is the thing for you.

The scariest thing I researched was the average savings in the UK. In July 2018, the average savings per person was only £5,582, and I read a report that on average, every person in the UK goes a further £800 into debt just to get through Christmas. This is why we're in Generation Rent – we're getting further and further away from ever being able to save a deposit to buy a house. Savings are getting harder to make. House prices are getting higher and higher. If you want to get onto the property ladder, if you want to build a scalable business, you need to use the No Money Down techniques. And not only that, I'm going to share with you a strategy that can help first-time buyers get on the property ladder: Rent2Own or Rent2Buy.

Have you heard of the government's Help to Buy scheme? They introduced it to try and help get people on the property ladder, and it had the effect of pushing house prices up even further. The average age of a first-time buyer in the UK in July 2018 was 37; in London and the South East it's mid-50s and rising all the time. The reality is it's easy to make money from property, so wouldn't it be great to make the money while helping people at the same time? You can help first-time buyers through your very own Rent2Own scheme; more on this later.

My Eastern European adventure left me not only with no money, but also with massive debt, so learning and implementing these strategies was an easy choice for me – it was my only choice, as there was no way I could ever have earned my way out of my debt in a day job. I speak at a lot of property events around the world, and people always come up to me saying No Money Down is not for them, as they "have money". But you know what, they've kind of missed the point – I am lucky enough to have money now, but I still don't use it to invest. The thing about money is if you keep spending it or investing it in property, you will eventually run out. If using your own money is your only method of buying property, then when, and not if, you run out, you will be stuck!

Those of you reading this book who have some investment properties will know too well that four or five houses is not enough to get to financial freedom. My first six properties gave me a passive income of on average £1,800 per month (up and down depending on repairs); £1,800 might sound like a lot to you right now, but it's not enough to get you out of your job. The most important thing in life is not money, it's what you can do with the money that's important!

My initial aim was to replace my salary; my take home pay was £2,750 per month so I planned to quit my job when I got to £3,000 per month. It took me nine properties to get to that point – a mixture of single lets and houses in multiple occupation (HMOs). 99% of people will run out of money before they can save up enough for deposits to buy nine properties. I secured mine using lease options and Rent2Rents, which I will show you how to secure later in the book.

Here's the thing, when I hit my initial target of £3,000 I didn't leave my job. The reason I didn't leave was fear – fear of things going wrong again, fear of losing everything I had built up, and feeling that the job gave me a little extra security. I would be walking away from my pension, free healthcare, life insurance policy and company car. These are really the chains that corporate companies put on you to keep you where you are. I still have all these 'benefits' today, but they are paid for using other people's properties, which I control through Rent2Rent agreements. In the end, I doubled my target – i.e. £6,000 before I quit – and here's where it got interesting" I doubled my income within the next six months.

"I'm working full-time on my job and part time on my fortune. But it won't be long before I'm working full-time on my fortune… can you imagine what my life will look like?"
– Jim Rohn

It took me 10 years to get to £1,800 per month, a further nine months to get to £3,000 and just another six months to get to £6,000. WHY? Because I was getting better! The Golfer Gary Player once said, "the harder I practice the luckier I get" and the same is true for anything; it wasn't that I got lucky, I just got better. We live in a world of instant gratification today; most people plan to take over the world within six months, and when it doesn't happen, they quit and move onto the next get rich quick idea, repeating the same behaviours over and over again and wondering why nothing works for them. That was me, too, in my first 10 years in property – I tried lots of different things in and outside of property and I felt none of them worked for me. The reality is nothing works unless you work and put enough time into making it work. If you're reading this book because you want a get rich quick strategy, I'll save you some time: you can put this book down and do something else. There is no such thing as get rich quick, unless you win the lottery or get left a large inheritance. What this book is about is taking consistent steps to move you forward, and if you follow the steps, you will get rich. Some will do it quicker than others, but if you stick to it, you will all make it in the end. Warren Buffet was once asked what the secret to his success was and his response was: "I've just been doing it longer than everybody else". If you implement the strategies in this book and play the long game, you will get very rich slowly.

What are the No Money Down (NMD) strategies?

There are 14 different No Money Down strategies that can either be used independently to do a property deal or in combination on the same property deal. To make it easy to follow, I have designed the No Money Down Matrix, which shows each of the strategies. I will talk through each one in detail throughout this book, explaining the strategy, how it works, when to use it, the risks and benefits to be aware of and some deal examples to show you how you can use each strategy.

The No Money Down Matrix

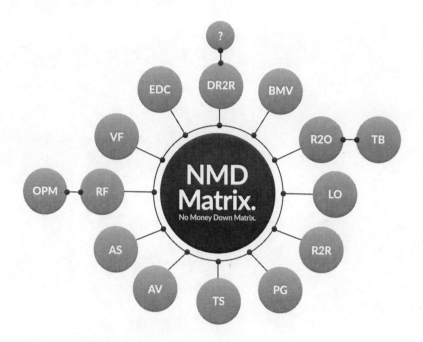

LO:	Lease Option
R2R:	Rent2Rent
R2O:	Rent2Own
TB:	Tenant Buyers
AV:	Adding Value
TS:	Title Split
PG:	Planning Gain
VF:	Vendor Finance
EDC:	Exchange with Delayed Completion
OPM:	Other People's Money
AS:	Assisted Sales
BMV:	Below Market Value
AP:	Adverse Possession
DR2R:	Don't Rent2Rent

Chapter 2: What Area Should You Invest In?

We are going to cover lots of different investment strategies in this book, but first let's look at what area you should invest in. The answer is very simple: YOUR AREA. I'm constantly meeting people who tell me there are no deals in their area, they can't do property where they live and that they are going to start investing, or worse still have already started investing, in an area over two hours' drive away. It is quite often an area they have never been to before or had never been to until they started to invest there. This just doesn't make sense. For most people the whole point of getting into property in the first place is to free them from their jobs, not to create a second job. If you have to travel over two hours every time you want to do a viewing or see your properties, what you are really doing is creating a second job.

It takes years to learn an area well enough to invest there; I moved north from Grays in Essex to north Nottinghamshire in 2009, and I didn't really get moving on my property journey there until 2014, partly because I didn't know my area. Now I know what streets in my area are the best for each different investment strategy – you wouldn't refurbish a house to flip for a profit on the same street as you would buy an HMO, and you wouldn't buy an HMO on the same street as you would buy a single let. I see investors from outside of the area coming in and buying properties on certain streets that I wouldn't touch because I know the area, but they see the house is cheap and on paper has a good yield. I learnt an expensive lesson in my first couple of years investing in property, and that lesson was that cheap does not necessarily mean valuable, cheap just means cheap. You might be able to get a house very cheaply, but then when you go to collect the rent you either get shot or stabbed.

I don't want you to create a second job, I want you to be free from your jobs so that you have the time to live life on your terms, doing what you want to do when you want to do it. So, let's look at how property will work in your area, within a 15-45 minute drive from where you live. There are strategies that will work in your area but there are also strategies that won't. The thing is, far too often people focus on what won't work and talk themselves out of investing, instead of identifying what will work and putting all their energy and focus into being the go-to person for that strategy in their area.

When I say a 15-45 minute drive from where you live, it needs to be an area with at least 50,000 houses. Let me tell you why: it's not that people don't rent in smaller areas, or that you can't make some strategies work in smaller areas, but more because if you want to be able to scale your business and build a large portfolio, you need to have a decent sized housing stock to work with. A housing stock of 50,000 is a nice size; if you purchased 100 houses in an area with a housing stock of 50,000, that would be 0.2% of the houses, which would still leave plenty for the competition and homeowners.

So what strategy did I pick in my area? I started by focussing on what other investors in the area were doing; if one other person is making money from property in your area then you can too. The biggest mistake most people make is they see a successful investor and think to themselves, *ok, they are doing X so I must avoid that and do Y* – NO NO NO! Follow the successful and success follows. Do exactly what they are doing – if the competition are using a certain strategy and making money from it then you can too, they are using that strategy because it works, there is enough room for everyone.

Now when I say follow the successful, I mean in your local area, I don't mean travelling across the county to invest in an area just because you saw someone you perceive to be a successful investor doing deals in that area.

Following other investors to towns and cities you don't know and buying properties on streets you don't know just because you "heard it was a good area" or "a person who teaches X strategy invests there" is one of the biggest mistakes I see people making when starting out in property. You cannot compete with investors in an area you don't know; I know my area better then you, but on the reverse side, you know your area better than me. You know the good streets, the bad streets, the high crime areas, and the areas where people aspire to live. You cannot beat local knowledge. I find a lot of my deals direct to vendor and I will show you the main marketing techniques I use to attract motivated sellers in chapter 6. But let's say you use the very same marketing techniques as me and we get a call from the same vendor; you won't be able to compete with me on the deal if you live over two hours away, because by the time you get off the phone, get fuel in the car and set off I'll already have been to the house to meet the vendor, had a cup of tea or coffee and secured a deal. You must work local to where you live, find the strategy that works in your area and you will make massive money.

Now I know some of you reading this book will be thinking *single lets don't work in my area* and you are likely to be right, but if they don't then strategies like assisted sales, commercial conversions or HMOs might. However, one of the other major mistakes I see people doing is picking a strategy that they like and trying to make it fit in the area they want to invest in; that's like trying to fit a square peg in a round hole. You have to reverse engineer the process: find the strategy that works in your area and take massive action to learn and implement that strategy. Every single property investment strategy can be done using No Money Down Investment techniques – don't think you are limited to one strategy because you don't have any money or very little money. Stop focussing on the money and start focussing on learning No Money Down Investment techniques and finding deals.

Would you buy a house on this street?

Have you spotted the horse? At various events I've spoke at over the last few years I've asked people in the audience if they would buy a house on this street, and once they notice the horse there is usually a 50-50 split between people who raise their hands to say they would and people who say they wouldn't. What every single person is doing is basing their financial future, their livelihood, on their perception of a horse. I took this picture while standing outside the front door of a single let property I had just secured a lease option on; lease options are one of the No Money Down strategies I will be covering later. The house we secured was on the market for quite a while and nobody bid on it, and the main reason nobody bid was because of the horse. But I knew something about that horse that other people didn't know: I knew that that horse had legs. You see, if I stood there today and took that same picture, the horse would be gone but the property would still be there; the horse allowed me the opportunity to structure a creative deal with the homeowner. The horse was never going to be there forever but the house will be there for years to come.

It's often little things that put people off buying a property – colours of walls or carpets, size of gardens, perception of a horse – but as a professional property investor, you have to know your area, base your decision on the numbers and not get emotional. You have to know your area better than anyone else and that's why investing locally to you is so important. I know that some out of town investors looked at this property, chose not to buy it because of the horse and then bought on the wrong streets because the house prices were lower and there was no horse. In reality they ended up buying in a worse area; you cannot compete with local knowledge.

You know your area better than me. I know my area better than anybody. You need to know your area not just better than me but better than anyone else locally as well. It will take you three to five years to learn another area. You can go up north, or you can go five hours away, and pick a house where you won't know what you are buying, and you'll be basing your investment decision on the numbers. You should be investing within 45 minutes of your home and basing your investment decision on actual value and actual statistics.

The Bronx v Manhattan

Have you heard of the Bronx to Manhattan analogy? This is used when analysing an area to identify where the best places are to buy single let Buy2Let properties.

Can I give you the Bronx to Manhattan analogy in a completely different way?

In every town you've got your Bronx, which is the streets where you can buy the cheapest properties, and you have also got a Manhattan type area where the properties are the most expensive. I bet as I'm saying this you're starting to think of these areas in your town. When identifying your single let Buy2Let area, the best yields will always be achieved in the cheapest areas – for example, if you go to the cheapest streets in my area, you can still buy a house for about £50,000 that would rent out for about £375 a month, giving a yield of 9% per annum (£375 x 12 months divided by £50,000 = 9% yield), which is quite good. However, you will likely have tenant issues as well as higher rent arrears and more voids than you would in a higher demographic area. On the reverse side, if you buy a property in one of the more expensive streets in my area, let's say you can buy a property for about £300,000 in an area that would score an 8 on the graph and that will rent out for £750 per month; this only gives a yield of 3%, which means you wouldn't have enough profit to pay the mortgage if you were buying it as a Buy2Let.

So now let's look at the middle of the graph, the areas that would score between 5 and 8. This is what I call suburbia: the nice newbuild properties (built in the last 5-20 years) with a drive and single/double garages, which have a lot of owner occupiers. If you get a Buy2Let property in these areas, the tenants will generally be a couple, both of whom work, want to live in a nice area and aspire to be homeowners – their friends live in these types of houses and they have a 'keep up with the Joneses' mentality. They want to be homeowners and have a short-term view of renting. Do they look after your property as well as somebody who wants it as a lifetime home? No, they don't!

The lifetime tenant wants to look after your property because they see it as their home. The short-term tenant who aspires to be a homeowner just sees your property as a rental property that they plan to leave as soon as they can afford to buy, so they don't look after it as well. But even worse is that every six to 18 months they leave because they found the dream home they wanted to buy, or could afford to buy, and now you've got voids.

This means that as well as having a lower yield due to it being a more expensive area, you also now have no rental income at all for periods of time, as tenants move out and you've got to find new tenants.

Therefore, the best places to buy single let Buy2Lets are just outside the cheapest areas (around the 2-4 areas on our scale), where you can get good quality tenants who will look after the property, pay the rent on time and have an ambition to be a renter for years to come, meaning you get few to no voids. Now this is a great strategy if you live in an area where property prices still give a good return on single lets. However, it does limit how many deals you can do and the types of properties you can invest in. Using No Money Down Investment techniques like lease options, Rent2Own and assisted sales allows you to play the property game wherever you choose on the 1-10 price graph, so wherever you live there is a strategy that works in your area. You see, single lets work best in the lower demographic areas as you get a higher yield, but if you try and do buy2flip in the lower demographic areas, you may not lift up the price enough in relation to the money you spent. For example, if you spent £15-20K to add a loft conversion to a house in a cheap area, you might only add £15-20K to the value of the property, but if you spent the same amount adding a loft conversion to a house in an expensive area, you would be likely to add £30-50K to the property.

Now let's look at tenant buyers for a moment. My research shows that tenant buyers want to move up the property ladder and own a home in a nice area of town, so often the best places to focus on the tenant buyer strategy are in the 5-8 range on the graph. If single let Buy2Lets don't give a good enough return in the 5-8 area where you live, then the great news is that tenant buyers start to work, as you get a monthly market rent PLUS a 'top up' that means these very same properties now give you a positive monthly cash flow. I'll cover this in detail in chapter 5 – Rent2Own.

The most successful property investors understand that there is a strategy that works in every area, but they also understand that not every strategy works in every area – they don't try and do the strategy they are most passionate about in an area where it doesn't work. Instead, they reverse engineer the process and focus on identifying what does work in their area, then build their strategy around that.

Personally, my investments have two different areas of focus:

- Souring properties in the lower demographic areas (2-4) to secure on lease options, Rent2Rents or using joint venture funding to keep long term

- Souring properties in the middle demographic areas (5-8) for tenant buyers and assisted sales.

How do I identify the different social demographic areas?

Start by looking at where people shop: is it Poundland or John Lewis? Are there good transport links nearby? Lots of factories? Private or public schools? Which schools have the best grades each year and which are the lowest on the school league tables? What type of property stock is there? Is it mainly streets of terraced houses or are there a lot of newbuild suburbia-type properties?

Plot everything on a map. When doing this, it's important to make sure you drive or walk the streets to get a good feel for the area – for instance, just identifying that there are a lot of parks and recreational space on a map does not necessarily mean that it's a higher demographic area. Driving past a park during the day and seeing lots of parents and kids does not necessarily mean it's a good area either – for example, there is one park near my investment area, if you drove by it during the day you'd see lots of parents with their children playing on swings, but then if you drove by the very same park again at 1am, you'd see a completely different park – it would be full of drug dealers and people sleeping rough. Had I just driven past at 2pm, I might have perceived it to be a much better area than it was. But the same goes for the reverse: just because there were drug dealers and rough sleepers there at 1am doesn't necessarily mean it's a bad area;

there are a lot of homeless people in Knightsbridge and that's still one of the most expensive areas in the UK. This analysis helps you determine what type of area it is, but it's not the only thing you must do.

It is all about Location, Location, Location. If you were going to invest in HMOs for students, you wouldn't do it in a town where there were no students. So don't look for property for any type of tenant before first researching what the demand for that type of tenant is. If your target market is students you need to look for properties near a university; if its blue-collar workers then you need to look in an area where there are a lot of factories.

If you're looking to buy, refurbish, refinance and convert properties to HMOs using joint ventures or private Investor funding, then you need to check with the local council planning department and HMO Officer before you purchase a property, as you might come unstuck due to planning issues like Article 4. For example, in an Article 4 area, a planning application may be required for a conversion or development that would have otherwise been permitted. You need to apply for planning permission and change of use to convert non-HMO properties to HMOs, and it's very likely that the planning permission won't be granted on the grounds that there is already a high density of HMOs in the area. Already licenced HMOs are not affected. Not every town has an Article 4 area, and in those that do, generally only part of the town is designated an Article 4 area. The law is different everywhere, so if you are planning to do any sort of change of use from what a property currently is to something else then the first thing you need to do is ring the planning department in your local council and find out what the specific laws are in your area. This only affects you if you are planning to do conversions and developments; if your main strategy is lease options, single lets or tenant buyers then you are not affected. This is why it is so important to identify what works in your area and then build your strategy around that, rather than doing what you want to do and realising too late that you can't do what you wanted.

Who else can help you determine the best areas to invest? What about the police? They know all the good and bad streets, where most of the crime happens, sometimes even who's responsible (even if they can't prove it). Lots of crime statistics are now available online for you to research, although nothing beats getting first-hand information from a real person. How about the Fire Service? They have a heat map identifying where most house fires occur; 80% of house fires occur in lower demographic council and private rented properties, so find out what streets the Fire Service go to for 80% of the fires and then don't invest there.

Use Google, search for tenant demand, unemployment rates, crime statistics, first-time buyer market, housing benefit rates, and what houses are selling and renting for in your area. Research your local council website. All this information, plus more, is available at the press of a button – and it's FREE.

Everything you need to become the most knowledgeable property person in your area is on Google and in your town. Walk into the police station and ask them. Walk into the fire station and ask them. Find out the information about your town; it's all there for you, you just have to go out and get it.

Chapter 3: Rent2Rent

There are lots of strategies that I will share with you that will let you build a portfolio of properties to leave a long-term legacy for generations to come, but your main focus starting out should be on cash flow – pure and simple cash flow to get you out of your job and give you the time and freedom to live life on your terms and do what you want to do, when you want to do it. I'm going to start with the ultimate cash flow system – Rent2Rent – because once you have the cash flow, you then have the time to focus on building a large property business. When I speak to most people starting out in property, they tell me they want to own a lot of houses. Here's the thing, I'm going to say something controversial: I don't think you do. I think that you think you want to own a lot of houses, but what you really want is lots of CASH! Now I can hear you saying to yourself, "NO, I want the houses" but be honest, is that because you believe that you need to own the house to make the cash? Would that be right? Well, in this chapter I'm going to show you that you don't need to own houses to make cash, you need to control the property to make the cash. Here's the problem: if you want to buy property to make the cash, the reality is 99% of people reading this right now are going to run out of money before they own enough houses to free themselves from their jobs. That is the reality! So let's start to focus on making some CASH!

A recent Nationwide quarterly spending report revealed that 41% of Brits (about four in 10 people) have less than £6.60 per day left to spend after paying household bills. A recent newspaper article revealed that money is so tight that 30% of people have missed vital payments in the past year. Around a quarter of people are regularly spending more than they earn – on average just over £1K each per year more expenditure than earnings. Times have changed; job security does not offer the same meaning as it did years ago, earnings have not kept up with inflation and most people are less than two pay packets away from major financial problems. If you follow the advice I was brought up with – which was go to school, get a good education, get a good job, have a pension for retirement and get a mortgage to own your own home – then the average person in Britain is at risk of financial difficulty at some point in the future.

What about your chances of becoming a millionaire? The average UK salary in 2017 was £27,000 per annum (£21,741 after tax). That's £2,250 per month before tax, leaving a take-home pay after tax of £1,811.75. If you saved your entire salary of £1,811.75 every month for 45 years (not investing or taking interest into account), you would save £978,345 (£21,741 per year x 45 years). Less than a million pounds. And that's without eating, drinking, buying clothing, putting a roof over your head – without spending a single penny. This is the reason only the top 1% of earners have any chance of earning their way to becoming a millionaire. If you want to become a millionaire, you need to be investing, and property has historically proven to be the best investment vehicle. Now, if you want to get to a million pounds quickly then the quickest way is not only to use property as your investment vehicle, but to control other people's property as well as owning your own.

You need to start thinking completely differently if you want to guarantee not only financial stability, but also financial opulence. The most successful investors on earth focus on control. Rent2Rent is all about control and cash flowing someone else's property, and if you follow the steps in this book it can get you out of your job in the next six months. Note what I said there: it will not make you a millionaire in six months, but it will get you out of your job.

If I was offered the choice today of £1M in cash or £10K per month cash flow for the rest of my life, I would pick the £10K cash flow every single time. The thing about £1M today is it's not actually a lot of money, and you'll just spend it; most lottery winners end up going broke because they don't know how to handle money. But 10, 15, 20 grand a month will completely change your life! Cash flow is king; cash flow is what we need to be chasing; cash flow is what will completely change your life.

Had you heard of Rent2Rent before you picked up this book? Can you think of anyone you know either personally or in property communities who has done Rent2Rent deals? If the answer is yes to both questions, and you're are not doing it yet, then why not? There are usually a few reasons.

Reason one is that you don't know how. Well the good news is I'm going to show you how. Reason two is that you perceive it as too management-intensive and you don't want to create a second job. This is not about creating a second job, it's about freeing you from your job. I'm not busy managing tenants, it's all about having the right systems in place to manage the tenants for you. Rent2Rent is no more management-intensive than Buy2Rent – it's the systems you implement that are the key. You could hire one member of staff to look after all of your properties using the profit from a single Rent2Rent deal! You wouldn't even have to hire them full time, you could hire them on a commission basis for certain criteria and certain targets: they would get commission if rooms were filled and rents were paid. Reason three is that it's not their strategy! They think to themselves, I've heard of Rent2Rent but it's not my strategy, I am focusing on something else.

I want you to ask yourself a question before you read any further: ask yourself if the reason you are not doing Rent2Rent is because your focus is another strategy. Now ask yourself how long you have been doing that something else; are you getting results or are you still in your job?

If you have been doing something else, maybe for nine months, one year, two, even five years, but you are still in your job, you need to question what you're doing. Because here's the reality: if the reason you're not doing Rent2Rent is that you want to do something else, and you've been doing something else for years yet you're still not out of your job, the reality is whatever else you're doing is not working. So why don't you have a serious think about Rent2Rent as a strategy?

Look at how quickly you can get out of your job and once you have the time and freedom, you can do the things you are passionate about, while continuing to scale your Rent2Rent business, as it is a business that continues to grow.

We've now got so many Rent2Rent properties that we have set up our own letting agency. Remember, the wealthiest people have multiple streams of property income. We now have a letting business that is aligned with our property business. Would you like to do that? You can. Absolutely everyone reading this book can. All you must do is follow what everyone else is doing; follow a proven system and success follows.

What is Rent2Rent?

What is Rent2Rent and how do you get started? When a landlord has an investment property and they want to rent it out, where do most landlords go to find tenants? A letting agency, right? They then sign a management agreement with the agents, and the agents market the property and find a tenant for the landlord. The tenant pays the rent to the agents and the landlord gets the rent less the agents fees, plus any maintenance costs. If the agent can't find a suitable tenant, the property sits empty and the landlord makes no money. With Rent2Rent, you are offering the landlord guaranteed rent for his property every single month for an agreed timeframe (typically three to five years but can be any period of time) where they get paid whether the property is tenanted or not and you usually cover all of the maintenance and management costs and give the house back at the end of the agreed term in the same or better condition than you received it in. During the period of the contract, you rent the property out and benefit from the difference between the rental income you receive less the bills and payment to the landlord. Basically, all you are doing is replacing the word buy in Buy2Rent with the word rent; everything else is pretty much the same in terms of costs, and you save by not having to come up with a large deposit to buy and not needing to qualify for a mortgage. You can Rent2Rent anything – single let houses, HMOs, serviced accommodation

(SA), shops, commercial units, etc. – literally whatever strategy you were looking to buy properties with, you can rent them instead and then make money by renting them on to other people and sitting in the middle.

Is this not subletting, I hear you say? In a word, NO. Subletting is when someone agrees to rent a property from someone else under the perception that they will be living in it themselves, signs an Assured Shorthold Tenancy Agreement (AST) and then sublets it to someone else without the knowledge or consent of the letting agent or landlord. You are not subletting, you are effectively taking the place of the letting agent and have a management agreement, lease agreement or company let agreement similar to the management agreement a letting agent has with a landlord. The only difference is the wording of the agreement, which states that you are guaranteeing the rent rather than charging a management fee.

You need to be upfront with the landlord or agent and ensure they are fully aware of what the property will be used for. There are two key things that you need to ensure are in place so that you are complying with legislation and mortgage terms if the property has a mortgage. These are as follows:

- Whatever use you have planned for the property, e.g. HMO or SA, you need to ensure you have advised the homeowner that they need the consent of their lender to let the property under that use. If a property is already on a Buy2Let mortgage, then you would be able to let it as a single let. If it is already a licenced HMO then you can let it as an HMO. If the property is unencumbered, i.e. mortgage-free, then you can let it out using any strategy, with the agreement of the landlord.

- Whatever strategy you plan to use the property for, you need to ensure that the homeowner's buildings insurance covers them for that type of letting.

Before entering into an agreement, you should always speak to your local council to find out what you can and cannot do with a specific house in a certain area. I could tell you a list of things you can and cannot do, but unfortunately, it's not a one-size-fits-all thing; councils across the country can make their own criteria regarding what they will and will not allow, and in some cases, such as with HMOs, you may be required to have an HMO licence. Legislation changes yearly, so if I list specifics here they may be out of date in a month's time, or certainly by the time you read the book. With HMOs there are minimum requirements across the UK when it comes to licencing, but then there are additional extras depending on the council. The current minimum requirements for mandatory HMO licencing are:

- If a property is occupied by five of more people, which make up two or more households: A household is classed as an immediate family (parents and children), partners (married, civil partnership or co-habiting), or individuals.

- Properties above commercial buildings (such as shops or restaurants) must also be licensed.

This law used to be five or more people on three or more floors, but it is now simply five or more people in a property – floor numbers no longer matter. But in addition to this, there are some councils that have introduced Selective Licensing. Selective Licensing is a legal power under the Housing Act 2004 which allows local councils to introduce a requirement for private landlords in certain areas (determined by each council) to hold a licence for all rental properties, even single lets.

There are also certain areas within some council boroughs that come under an Article 4 Direction; this serves to restrict permitted development rights; if you are looking to agree a Rent2Rent on a property in an Article 4 area that is not currently a licenced HMO, then you would need planning permission to change its use and it's likely the application would be rejected.

I have mentioned all of the above to make you aware of different requirements and to ensure you understand that you cannot just take any house and do whatever you want with it, you need to ensure you adhere to the requirements of your local council. What I recommend you do is either ring your local council and ask to speak to the HMO officer or arrange a meeting with them to find out exactly what the requirements are in your area (if they don't have an HMO officer, then this job is usually covered by someone in the environmental health department).

In addition to local council licensing requirements, there is also UK health and safety law. For instance, with an HMO, in certain areas you may not require a licence; however, if you rent rooms out to unrelated people and don't fit fire doors or a smoke alarm system (fire alarm systems may be required in larger properties – again find out what the requirements are from your local HMO officer), and one of the tenants falls asleep at night with a lit cigarette and burns the house, killing another tenant, you may be at risk of being charged with manslaughter. This is because under health and safety law you have a duty of care to do all that is reasonably practicable to keep your tenants safe. I'm not saying this to scare you and put you completely off investing in property, I'm saying this because it would be wrong of me to only share all the benefits with you and not the risks. It winds me up when I read books or attend trainings and the 'expert' teaching the strategy only shares the positives. With any strategy there are risks and rewards, and none of what I have just mentioned is difficult to implement to ensure you not only make a lot of money but also do so while protecting yourself from the risks.

When determining how many bedrooms you can get from an HMO, you need to be aware of the minimum bedroom sizes allowed – this is covered under Schedule 4 of the Housing Act 2004; again, always check with your local council to ensure you know what the latest rules are. At this time the current rules are:

- For a room to be considered a bedroom it needs to be a minimum of 6.52 square meters, so if it is smaller than 6.52 square meters you will not be allowed to rent it out to an individual person.

- Rooms between 6.52 square meters and 10.22 square meters can only be let to individuals and not couples.

- If you want to rent to a couple, then the room must be a minimum of 10.23 square meters.

The rules do not apply to visitors who are staying for a short time; we have in our contracts that anyone not named on the contract who is staying three nights or less in a tenant's room is considered a guest and if they are there for four or more nights then they are a tenant. If they are a tenant, they are to be named on the tenancy agreement and pay rent, and the room should be an adequate size for two people to share. Children are also counted in this instance, as the rules refer to people and not adults.

All of this legislation and the changes are a massive opportunity for the educated property investor to cash in on other people's fear. As Warren Buffet said, "Be fearful when others are greedy and greedy when others are fearful".

Why doesn't the landlord just rent it themselves?

I would say the most common question, and one of the first questions I get asked at my live training events, is "why doesn't the landlord just rent their own house out if there is so much money in it?" My response is always "Why do letting agents exist?" Why do landlords give their properties to letting agents when they could just rent them out themselves? The answer is simple: Because they don't want to. Most people don't ever learn the strategies you will read about in this book, they want the income that an investment property gives without the perceived hassle of managing them. Often, people just want to stay in their jobs and have some extra income from property. All the reasons why someone would give their property to a letting agency to manage are the very same reasons why they would also give the property to you to manage. You see, they're not deciding whether to give it to you or do it themselves, they're deciding whether to give it to you or to the letting agency.

Let's look at the difference between Rent2Rent and letting agents from a landlord's perspective:

1. Letting agents charge them a management fee to manage the property, usually a percentage of the monthly rental income received.

2. If the property is empty they don't get charged, but they also don't make any money.

3. Letting agents generally charge a tenant finding fee every time they source a new tenant.

4. Letting agents generally charge for renewing contracts every 6-12 months.

5. If there are any maintenance issues, the landlord is responsible for the costs, and if the repairs are organised by the letting agency they may also charge an admin fee.

That's a whole lot of fees coming out of the monthly rent from just one property! With Rent2Rent you are offering:

1. Guaranteed rent so the landlord gets paid even if the property is empty.

2. No management or tenant finding fees.

3. No voids.

4. No maintenance (we typically agree to pay for internal and cosmetic maintenance plus maintaining the gardens and the landlord covers structural issues).

The rent you offer will be slightly lower than the rent they would get from a letting agency but more than the net amount they would actually put in their pocket after all agency's costs were deducted.

Let's look at a typical scenario:

	Letting agency	Rent2Rent
Market rent	£1,000	£850
Annual rental income	£12,000	£10,200
Annual management fee – 10% +Vat	£1,440	£0
Typical void period	- £1,200 (10%)	£0
Typical repairs costs	-£1,000	£0
Annual gas and electric certs	-£100	£0
INCOME LANDLORD RECEIVES	£8,260	£10,200
Income over 5 years	£41,300	£51,000

This landlord is financially better off by £1,940 per year (£161.66 per month) with Rent2Rent than if they were to let the property via letting agents, even though they are receiving £150 per month less in market rent.

The above doesn't even include costs of tenant finding fees and admin fees, but it still clearly shows a landlord is financially much better off agreeing to guaranteed rent, and there are no hidden costs or worries about things like non-paying tenants that could significantly increase the landlord's costs.

Even though it's a lower monthly figure, is the guaranteed rent a better deal for the landlord? Absolutely! Also, right now is the perfect storm for Rent2Rent because of the changes to legislation, which mean letting agencies will no longer be able to charge tenants fees. In a typical letting agency, tenant fees account for around 30-35% of turnover, so when they can no longer charge fees, their business model becomes unsustainable. This means they are going to need to adapt to survive and one of the most likely ways to replace the lost revenue will be to charge landlords even more, making your guaranteed rent offer even more appealing to landlords.

You now take the property where you have agreed guaranteed rent with the landlord and multi-let it, either as an HMO or SA.

Let's look at an HMO:

Purchase price (if you were to buy):	£200,000
Achievable rent per room:	£450 pcm
Number of bedrooms:	5
Achievable rent for house	£450x5 = £2,250
Rent to landlord:	£850
Bills:	£500
Total costs:	£850 + £500 = £1,350
Profit:	£2,250 - £1,350 = £900 pcm

Let's look at an SA:

Purchase price (if you were to buy):	£200,000
Achievable rent per night:	£100
Achievable rent per year at 70% occupancy	£19,710 (£100x365days = £36,500 /100*70% = £25,550)
Achievable rent per month at 70% occupancy	£2,129.17 (25,550/12months)
Rent to landlord:	£850
Bills:	£600
Total costs:	£850 + £600 = £1,450
Profit:	£2,129.17-£1,450 = £679.17 pcm

The HMO scenario, in which the landlord is financially better off by £161.66 per month, also gives you a profit of £900 per month – and you don't have to come up with a large deposit to purchase the property (typically 25% of purchase price = £50K deposit not required).

One of the things I love most about the Rent2Rent strategy is it works everywhere. If you are looking to do Rent2Rent HMOs, I wouldn't recommend doing it in towns with a population of less than 50,000 people, as there needs to be enough room to scale. And even though it works well in any location with more than 50,000 people, it works unbelievably well in larger cities where it is expensive to live due to supply and demand.

If you are in an area with fewer than 50,000 people, or in an area where the council won't allow any more HMOs such as Article 4 areas, then you can either target already licenced HMOs in the Article 4 areas or do SA in these areas and the smaller towns.

Pay yourself first

Have you heard the saying pay yourself first? The rich live by this principal, and with Rent2Rent you literally can pay yourself first. If you were to buy a property and then look to rent it out, you would need to come up with the deposit funds, purchase fees such as solicitor costs and stamp duty, and that's a list of outgoings before any money comes in. With Rent2Rent, you can calculate what your profit is before you take on the deal. I follow a very simple rule to ensure I never take on a deal that could lose me money: the rule of 1.5.

People regularly contact me or attend my events AFTER they have already attempted to do Rent2Rent on their own and tell me they are losing money but are stuck in a contract they can't get out of. One particular example was a lady who had taken on a Rent2Rent deal in London where she was making £700 per month profit from one house. On the face of it, that sounds brilliant, but the problem was each room rented for £900 per month and she only made £700 profit if the house was full; with one room empty, her £700 profit turned into a £200 loss, which is not good!

Every deal you take on needs to be profitable, and you must expect periods where you will have rooms empty. We target an occupancy rate of 96%

across our portfolio, which means for every 100 rooms you will have four empty. Now if there are five rooms in each house and you have 100 rooms, that's 20 houses, agreed? So, if you have 20 houses and you have one empty room in four of the houses, and one empty room means you lose money, then you are effectively now losing money on 4/20 properties – this is not a good business model. The rule of 1.5 protects you, enabling you to pay yourself first and calculate the maximum rent you can afford to pay a landlord.

How the rule of 1.5 works:

Let's take the earlier example where the achievable monthly rent for a room was £450 and there were five bedrooms. To pay yourself first, you use the rule of 1.5, which is the achievable rent for 1.5 bedrooms, i.e. £450 + £225 (half the achievable rent for bedroom two) = £675

Total rent achievable:	£450 x 5 rooms = £2,250
Pay yourself first:	£450 x 1.5 rooms = £675
Then pay the bills:	£500

Now deduct the £675 + £500 from the total achievable rent:

£2,250-£675-£500 = £1,075. This means £1,075 is the maximum amount you can afford to pay the landlord monthly as a guaranteed rent. The average costs of bills over 12 months will stay pretty much the same, so every pound less than £1,075 per month you negotiate to pay the landlord is added to your £675 profit.

Most importantly, the rule of 1.5 ensures that even if you have one room empty, you are still making a profit for 50% of room two.

The rule of 1.5 works for houses of four to six people. I don't recommend doing HMOs on houses with one to three bedrooms. For houses with more than seven people, use £125 per room profit to pay yourself first.

1-3-bed properties:	Rent2Rent for SA
4-6-bed properties:	Rent2Rent for HMO using the rule of 1.5 to calculate your profit and what to pay the landlord
7+-bed properties:	Rent2Rent for HMO using £125 per room profit to calculate your profit and what to pay the landlord

The rule of 1.5 ensures you make a monthly profit but it doesn't protect you from spending too much money initially on setting the deal up. If you get to the real root of why you invest in property, it's to make a profit, to make CASH! So if you are spending too much cash on acquiring the property in the first place, it will take you years to get your cash back; this is where the six month rule comes in. I never take on a Rent2Rent deal unless I can get all of my money back out within the first six months, meaning that by month seven I'm making a profit. I'm not talking about a fantasy profit where, for example, people leave £50,000 of their life savings in a deal and then make £500 a month cash flow and call it profit. I'm talking real profit, where you get all of your initial investment back out in the first six months and then the monthly profit is true profit making your return on investment infinite.

How does the six month rule work? If you take the deal discussed earlier, in which your monthly positive cash flow was £900, you take the £900 and multiply it by six months, giving you £5,400. What this means is that the maximum you can spend on refurbishing the property is £5,400 – if you spend more than this, it will take you longer than six months to get your money back out, and that is risky. It scares me when I see people spending £20-30K on a Rent2Rent deal that only makes a few hundred pounds per month profit... it's not your house!

We are not in the business of improving and managing other people's properties for nothing, we are in the business of making CASH.

If you find an ideal property but it needs more than six months' rental profit to get it ready to let then this doesn't mean you can't do the deal, what it means is that the six months' rental profit is the maximum you can put into the deal. You could negotiate with the landlord for them to invest the rest – at the end of the day, it is their house.

Note: I'm talking about monthly rental income profit here, after landlord payment and bills have been deducted; don't confuse this with rental income or you will spend too much.

Securing deals via letting agents

You can source deals either direct to vendor or via letting agents, I will be covering marketing for deals via estate agents and direct to vendor in chapter 6, but I want to cover some techniques here that are specific to Rent2Rent via letting agents.

- I know we have been talking about Rent2Rent up to this point, but the most important thing to remember is NEVER EVER call it Rent2Rent when speaking to a letting agent – it's corporate letting. Agents understand corporate letting but they don't understand Rent2Rent – they see it as subletting.

- Be yourself but be confident – people invest in people and, no matter what you may have heard, letting agents are human after all.

- Never pitch to an agent over the phone – it's too easy for them to dismiss you and say no. Go and see them or book some viewings so you get to know them, and they get to know you. People want to see who they are doing business with, and they will want to work with serious investors; serious investors make the time to build relationships

- Practice with 10 agents out of town – the worst mistake you can do is to visit the most important or closest agents to your investment area first. Why? Because you're not an expert yet, you need to practise! The first few times you visit an agent, I guarantee you will say something wrong or mess it up, so practice out of town, and once you have perfected your pitch, then go to your investment area and pitch to your most important agents.

- Do your research before you visit – make sure you know what properties rent for and what areas you are looking to get properties in.

- Be very clear on what it is you are offering and get to the point; if you don't know, then how can you explain it clearly? Practise your pitch before you visit any agents. Letting agents are busy, but also, if you are beating about the bush and not explaining exactly what you are offering, the letting agents will see through it. Say you are looking to take on a few properties in the next one to two months – this means more commission for the agents if they can do more than one deal with you. And remember, perception is reality: if you come across as confident and knowing what you are talking about, they will be more open to working with you.

- Name drop some big employers in the area that you are looking for houses for to accommodate their employees on a medium to long-term basis.

- Don't panic if a letting agent says no to you; even when you become competent at Rent2Rent, you still won't get every letting agent to agree to work with you. The good news is you don't need them all to work with you, you actually just need one! One agent can bring you enough deals to change your financial future forever. No matter how many noes you get, never give up – the only way you can fail in property is if you quit!

- Be very clear on the benefits to the letting agent and make sure you explain the benefits to them. Be careful here, though – don't teach them too much, otherwise they might think what you are discussing is a great idea and they could just do it themselves and no longer need you. Ask the agent what's most important to them. It might be reputation or ensuring the property gets let quickly, it might be that they maintain control of the property or ensuring rent is always paid in full and on time, or it might simply be CASH. Often money talks, and if you can, show the agent how they can make as much money as they would from a traditional let (or more money), without the hassle of having to manage the property. Listen carefully for what you think might be most important to the agent, structure your offer to solve this and you will be on to a winner.

- Don't be pushy and try to push what you want to do onto the agents; listen to what is most important to them and focus on solving that problem. Remember, we have two ears and one mouth, and they should be used in that proportion.

Remember: A lot of estate agents also do lettings, and often they advertise this badly, so always ask. There are also lots of online agents now, and these are a great way of getting direct to the landlord, as the online agents often don't do their own viewings. Then there are the smaller independent agencies that need to do a certain number of transactions in the month in order to pay their mortgage and put bread on the table; they can often be more open to corporate lets, especially if they are having a slow month in terms of commissions.

Some questions to ask the letting agents to determine if a deal will work and if they are open to working with you:

- Is the property still available to let?

- How long has it been on the market?

- Would the landlord be open to a longer-term contract?

- Do you do corporate lets, and if so, would the landlord of this property be open to a longer-term corporate let agreement?

- Can I arrange a viewing please?

Getting the property ready for little or no money

When you are negotiating a Rent2Rent deal, there are a number of potential costs that you want to aim to avoid. These are as follows:

- **Deposits:**
  You are a managing agent and managing agents do not pay landlords deposits, tenants pay deposits! Therefore, you should aim to avoid paying a deposit when possible. If this cannot be agreed and a deposit is required, then your aim is to get the landlord to agree to deposit protection insurance in lieu of a deposit.

- **Upfront rent:**
  We often negotiate an upfront rent-free period of anything from two to eight weeks, to allow us to get properties ready for letting and aim to get the first tenants in place before the first rental payment is due, so we can use rental income to pay the landlord.

- **Refurbishment:**
  Your starting point on all negotiations should be that the landlord pays for the refurbishment – after all, it is his property. Once he has refurbished it, you will guarantee the rent and cover all internal maintenance and return the property to him in as good or better condition. If this is not agreeable, then you can offer to cover some or all the refurbishment costs, as long as it still meets your criteria for profit from the deal.

- **Furniture:**

  There are companies available in the UK that you can lease furniture from – several of them advertise in Facebook property groups and speak at local networking events. Attend your local Progressive Property Network (PPN) event and ask the host about furniture leasing providers. They will lease you the furniture for a number of years and give you the option to then buy it for a token sum at the end of the term or replace it with new furniture on a new lease. This is a tax-deductible expense, but more importantly, it means you don't have to make a cash outlay upfront to furnish the property and the costs can then be paid monthly from rental income. However, should you choose to buy the furniture, I would recommend going to places like IKEA, which offer very good solid furniture at cheap prices – and you can pay monthly and, again, cover the cost from rental income.

- **White goods:**

  Items like fridge freezers, washer/dryers, TVs, irons, kettles, toasters, etc. can be purchased from Currys on a buy-now-pay-later agreement, again, allowing you to get the tenants in place and pay for the items 6-12 months later using profit from the rental income. You do need to spend some money to get a property ready for letting, but you can be creative about how you structure your white goods purchases and when you pay for them, so you can make your Rent2Rent deals No (own) Money Down.

Once you have got the property furnished and looking pristine it's time to get your tenants in place.

Finding and managing tenants

With Rent2Rent, you can either find and manage the tenant yourself or give the task to an agent to do for you. Even when looking at Rent2Rent SA, there are national SA management providers who will manage the full process for you on a commission basis.

However, you should be looking to grow your business to a point where it makes financial sense to manage the properties in-house by hiring staff to do it. When you are starting off, you can't afford staff full-time, but you can hire people part-time and on a commission basis. For instance, maybe your first three deals bring in a monthly positive cash flow of £1K per month each = £3K per month, which will free you from your job. You don't want to be creating a second job – you need to be working 'on your business' and not 'in your business' – so maybe you use the £1K profit from deal number four to hire a property manager part-time, who gets paid commission for each room that's filled and for rental income received. Be careful when offering commission-based incentives, though, as it can incentivise a person in the wrong way – for example, you agree to pay commission for finding tenants, but then the property gets filled with the wrong type of tenants, who either trash the house or don't pay the rent. Always make sure the commission is also based on the conduct of the tenants. I pay 50% of the commission if a house is over 94% occupancy in a month and the other 50% if the occupants of the house have paid 100% of the rent due in that period.

There are some real benefits to managing your properties in-house, such as:

- You (or your property manager) get to meet the prospective tenant face to face. Although credit checks and referencing are an important part of the process, seeing someone face to face allows you to get a feel for what type of tenant they will be.

- In shared houses, it's always good to see the reaction of the current tenants when the new person has been shown around – we always like to hang on after the viewing and ask the current tenants what they thought of the potential new person. You don't want to upset the household and risk losing good paying and tidy tenants by letting the wrong person in, but it's a fine balance and there will be some tenants whose opinion you won't want to ask, as they can find fault with anyone. Your gut feeling will guide you here.

- Getting to know your tenant on day one and making them feel at home is a critical part of a successful tenancy. Make sure the tenant knows that you are approachable and to make you aware of any issues immediately, no matter how small – picking up on minor maintenance issues early can save you a fortune in the long run, as issues only ever get bigger, they never go away.

- If you or your property manager meet the tenants at the property, you can answer the tenant's questions about the property, some of which a letting agent may not know the answer to.

- Although you want to build a relationship with the tenant, you don't want them to think they can take advantage, so always make sure they know who the boss is. Tenants can sometime try to take advantage of your kindness and availability so be firm but fair.

- Always ensure the property is clean and tidy before a viewing and inspect the property regularly.

- When possible, it's good to arrange more than one viewing at the same time or with a five-minute crossover, as tenants usually have other rooms to see and tend to not want to commit on the spot. If they like the room and see that other people are also viewing, then the fear of loss will push them to a decision there and then.

- Managing your own tenants in-house allows you to scale another business – you can hire more staff, open your own agency to the public and take on the management of other people's properties. The management fees from managing other people's properties pays for your staff and you get your properties managed for FREE.

Long term you could then look to franchise the agency and open new shops across the country.

Branding:

Branding your business is important but it's not critical to success! I see so many people use the fact they don't have a website or business cards yet as a reason why they can't visit a letting agency or do a viewing. I had done lots of deals before I ever had a website or business cards. Getting all these things in place is what I call getting your ducks in a row; a duck never made me any money, but viewings and offers have. Focus on viewings and offers! It's a numbers game – if you are viewing enough houses and make enough offers, you can't avoid deals.

Compliance:

As with any business, there are some areas of compliance that you need to be aware of. These are:

1. General Data Protection Policy (GDPR) is a regulation in EU law on data protection and privacy for all individuals within the European Union and the European Economic Area. Additionally, if you are handling other people's data, then you should be registered with the Information Commissioner's Office (ICO) – you can register by visiting their website, ico.org.uk.
   A guide to GDPR can also be found here: *https://ico.org.uk/for-organisations/guide-to-the-general-data-protection-regulation-gdpr/*

2. I would recommend registering with a dispute resolution service provider such as The Property Ombudsman.

You should also have professional indemnity insurance and public liability insurance. If you want some recommendations on where to get these, send me a message on social media or via my website, www.kevinmcdonnell.co.uk.

Systemising:

Systemising your business is a key to being able to scale and grow. There are an endless number of apps, systems and websites that can make pretty much every part of your business automated. The following are what I use but others are available:

- **Outsourcing:**

  In any business it's difficult to find time to do all the tasks that need doing and still be able to scale and grow – you can get bogged down in admin very quickly and hiring staff can seem expensive. There are lots of websites now, like PeoplePerHour, Fiverr, Upwork and so on, where you can hire virtual assistants to do pretty much anything you need doing for very little money, especially all those mundane admin tasks.

- **Property management software:**

  There are lots of different property management software systems on the market that can manage all of your tenants, maintenance, paperwork, reminders for renewals of gas safety checks, etc. all in one place. Two of the most popular are Arthur and Go Tenant!. When you are starting out, for your first few properties all you really need is an Excel spreadsheet, but as you grow you will need a property management system. Don't just pick the first one you see, trial some different ones out and pick the one that you and your team can work best with.

- **iZettle:**

  When you do viewings, it is really helpful to have a way to take payments there and then. Most people won't be carrying large quantities of cash in their pockets, so having a method of taking card payments is a must. Again, there are lots of different card payment services available on the market. The one I use is iZettle – with this system, payments are taken instantly, and you are only ever charged when there is a transaction, there is no monthly subscription fee.

- **Signable:**

  When I started out a few years ago, I had paper everywhere. The thing about paper is it needs to be filed, which takes up space, and unless you are super organised it can go missing. With Signable, you and your tenants can sign all your contracts online, saving you time, money and space.

- **Accounts:**

  The most dreaded word of every business owner: accounts. It's vitally important that you stay on top of your accounts and make sure you are recording all your expenses and not losing or forgetting about receipts; I'm sure none of us want to be paying any more tax than we really need to. There are lots of apps that allow you to scan your receipts immediately when you get them. Make sure that whatever app you use is one that your bookkeeper and/or accountant is happy to work with. One app I used to use was Receipt Bank, because it was compatible with my accountant's accountancy software, Xero. Now I just use Dropbox, as Dropbox is FREE (up to a certain limit). I hired a bookkeeper part-time from PeoplePerHour and gave them access to my Dropbox and she created a dedicated receipts folder. The minute I get a receipt, I scan it using the Dropbox app on my phone; my bookkeeper then takes the receipt from the shared Dropbox folder and uploads it to Xero (our accountancy software system – again, others are available). Once a month, I email the bookkeeper a CSV file of my bank account and they upload this to Xero and reconcile the transactions. You can also give your bookkeeper read only access to your online banking, so they can do this part of the process themselves. At the end of the year, the accountant then has everything they need for the company returns already compiled and ready for them to submit.

- **Evernote:**

  Evernote is brilliant for recording things like inspections of properties, inventories, etc. You can use Evernote to write notes, record videos, record voice notes and take pictures. You then have a very comprehensive report all in one place that you can then easily share with your staff.

- **Facebook:**

  I have a closed Facebook group for my staff where we keep each other informed of day-to-day issues and information, tag each other in on information relevant to a certain person, link to website info, etc. This is really simple to use and a brilliant way of sharing information and keeping a record of who was told something and when.

- **CRM systems:**

  customer relationship management (CRM) systems are used to share job tasks, client information, etc. There are numerous different systems available on the market, such as Podio, Insightly, Asana, Less Annoying CRM and Infusionsoft. Pick one that matches your budget but be aware that with some it can be difficult to impossible to move information to another platform, so if you are planning to grow then pick one that meets your growth expectations.

Case study: Direct to vendor deals

This is a text message from the seller of the house:

> Mum and dad are really interested about what we discussed. Are you free on tuesday to talk a little more about it and answer a couple of questions?
> Speak soon and enjoy your journey to Ireland
> Sarah x

> I can't do tuesday but could meet on Wednesday if that's ok?

Do I look like I'm busy in that text message? I'm off to Ireland, I said "can't do Tuesday, still in Ireland but I can do Wednesday". So, after the meeting I got this reply:

> Thankyou. Between me and you me and mum wants to work with you but mick wants to sell so he's the one to work on. Don't let him know I gave you a heads up

> Ok thanks :)
> The contract is generic and anything that you want changing can be changed to suit, it needs to be right for both of us

See in the message where she refers to Mick? Mick is the Dad... Property is not about houses, property is not about numbers, property is about people – it's a people business. I spent my first 10 years in property chasing the numbers, chasing the houses, chasing the deal, chasing the money. When you chase the money, you don't find it, what you do find is debt. When you solve other people's problems, you make the money.

The money automatically comes to you. Have you ever heard the saying 'you must give to receive'? So, when I went back to the house for the next meeting, I focussed on Mick, I focussed on solving Mick's problem. The situation was that the family had bought a bed and breakfast in the Lake District and they were moving there that week. The house that we were negotiating a deal on was in Nottinghamshire. Mick wanted to sell the house in Nottinghamshire and move to the Lake District, leave the money from the house sale in the bank and in five or six years move back to Nottinghamshire to retire and be able to buy another house. He didn't want to move back to the same house, he wanted to move back to a different house. Has he got a good plan? No! Why not? One simple word: INFLATION.

Inflation is the flaw in his plan. I didn't try to negotiate a crazy offer to buy his house below market value (BMV). What I did was explain to him that if he sells the house today, there's a chance that he won't be able to get back on the property ladder in five to six years due to the possibility that house prices will be much higher and inflation will have eroded his money in the bank. Now if we're honest, none of us know if house prices will be the same, lower or higher in the future, but one thing we do know is that there are micro markets in the UK. What that means is that house prices can go up, down or sideways but if they do they will move at the same rate in a micro market; Mick wanted to buy back into the market in the same area as his current house, so therefore the safest place for him to leave his money was in the brick and mortar of the property. He could then sell the house at the time he wanted to buy the new house. No matter what happened to the market, he would then be able to buy a like-for-like house. Once I explained this to him and showed him that the smart thing to do would be to keep the house, he was sold on the idea of Rent2Rent. We shook hands on a deal and the paperwork was signed a couple of days later. That house makes me £556.66 per month profit. Had I just focussed on the number rather than solving Mick's problem and showing him what was best for him, I would likely have lost that deal.

The numbers:

1. Number of bedrooms: 4

2. Agreed rent on five-year management agreement (pcm): £550

3. Achievable rent as HMO (pcm): £1,581.66

4. Bills (pcm): £475

5. Profit (pcm): £556.66

Not a massive profit, but £550 is still a lot of money and just five of these deals would replace the average salary in the UK.

Case study: Ria Jenkins & Emilio Mccalla - Rent2HMO

Property details:

- Licenced HMO, medium condition, close to the town centre and a hospital in the area
- Number of bedrooms: 8 but licenced to 7
- Max rental in current condition (pcm): £2,242

Deal details:

- Length of contract agreed: six months (due to condition we were unsure)
- Rent income (pcm): £2,242
- Rent to landlord (pcm): £850
- Bills (pcm): £362.10
- Profit (pcm): £1,029.90

The following are Ria's words:

This property was sourced direct to vendor through letters sent to landlords on the local HMO register. The landlord contacted us because she was very interested in what we had to offer, and as we explained more, she was very eager to meet with us.

The landlord is from London, which is over 100 miles away from her property. She already had someone managing her property, but she was not very happy with the service she was being provided, as her property was becoming increasingly run down.

We agreed to meet on a date that was best for her as she lived so far away. Upon viewing the property, we knew it would make a good Rent2Rent. The house is an 8-bedroom house, only licenced to 7. There is a large room downstairs that was being used as a spare room and a single room upstairs that was being used as a bedroom, so we decided it would be a good idea to use the larger room as a bedroom and the single room as the spare room, as we would get more rental income. The kitchen was in a rundown state. After viewing the property, we went home, worked out the figures and did a lot of market research. We then sent an email to the landlord with our offer of £850, which she was very happy with and accepted.

We then requested a second viewing of the property to fully assess the condition of the house. The kitchen was our main concern, and on the second viewing of the kitchen, we were grateful to see that it was old but a good clean would bring it up to standard to get the property let out. We had a good look around the bedrooms to see what was needed, i.e. paint, beds and wardrobes, etc. Thankfully, the large spare room downstairs had two beds and a wardrobe inside that were of good enough quality to be used. We bought some paint, which really helped to brighten up the bedrooms.

Our initial investment was £450, which means we recovered our investment in the first month of taking over the property and started making a positive cash flow right away. The negotiations for the property took very little time, about one or two weeks, and we were very happy with the outcome of the negotiations. Kevin supported us through this whole process, as busy as he is, he always finds time to reply to our messages and help in any way he can. We have learnt a great deal about property investing through his No Money Down Masterclass course.

We are going to extend the contract with the Landlord to five years once the initial six-month contract is up. We are also going to refurbish the kitchen when the contract has been renewed. Based on market research, we believe we can slightly increase rental income once the kitchen has been refurbished.

More importantly, this has given us the opportunity to showcase what I can offer to this landlord, which should hopefully lead to us slowly starting to take over other properties in the area under a similar arrangement, as we can now use this as a case study. We have started the process of looking for another Rent2Rent in the same area.

Chapter 4: Lease Options

Wouldn't it be great if you didn't need to use banks all the time and worry about all their lending qualification criteria? Well here is the good news: you don't need to take out your own mortgage to get control of property. Using lease options, you can control other people's mortgages – babysit them and cash flow the properties at the same time by renting them out.

In this chapter I will explain what a lease option is and how to use it. If you already have a good understanding of lease options, are you using your knowledge to do deals? Because to know and not to do is not to know! Knowledge is power, but only if you use the power; a lease option is probably the most powerful strategy available to you today.

Bank loans can be expensive, especially to set up, with all the legal fees and admin fees added to the loans.

I often hear people say they are waiting for the right time to get started in property, trying to time the market, waiting to see what happens with the government, saving up for their first deposit, etc. Whatever your concern is, here's the reality: if you wait until one perceived problem is resolved before you buy any property, then you will never get started because there will always be another perceived problem getting in your way. The longer you wait, guess what's happening? Nothing! And your life is passing you by – suddenly 10, 12 years have gone by and you've done nothing! What you have to do is always invest, always! Every year, every few months, every month, every week or every day, if possible – be consistently investing all the time.

When you buy or take control of a property, you make money, and using a strategy like a lease option you get the opportunity to 'try before you buy', meaning you can mitigate your risks. Buying a property is one of the most expensive investments you will ever make in your life, and it still amazes me today the number of people who do this with no training whatsoever;

you wouldn't try to fly a plane without a lesson. Even with training and due diligence, in property investing there is always that worry that you might not be able to find a tenant or maybe the property won't rent for as much as you hoped. With tools like lease options you don't need to invest your life savings into a property – you can get control of the property for as little as £1.00 and then only buy later once you know it is profitable.

The rich have a saying: "if it moves, flies or floats, you control it, you don't own it". Control is the key to massive growth in property, and a lease option is one of the most powerful tools to allow you to control and cash flow other people's properties. Success leaves clues; if you follow the successful you will get success. So, you should focus on controlling other people's properties with no need for a deposit. If you don't have enough money for a deposit right now, then a lease option is the investment tool for you to get you started in property.

It's not just the deposit you don't need, you also don't need to apply for and take out your own mortgage – you babysit the current owner's mortgage. If you cannot get a mortgage right now, then a lease option is the thing for you. With lease options, there is also no need for credit checks. If you've got a black mark on your credit file, maybe you were late with a payment in the past, or if you're worried about your credit report for any reason, with lease options that's not a problem: you're not applying for credit, you are taking on a debt that is already in place and using tenants or tenant buyers (more about these later) to service the debt, or you have the option to sell the property immediately for a profit.

There is often a perception that a lease option is a very complex strategy, but in reality, it is a simple process that absolutely anybody can do. How do I know it's a simple process? Because I do it, and I was probably one of the worst property investors in the world when I started.

I challenge you to find someone who was as stupid as I was when I started – I am someone who went off to eastern Europe, with no training whatsoever, and lost £135,000 I didn't even have on three properties that turned out to be either complete scams or completely valueless. If I can do this, then you can too.

It's a learnt skill, it doesn't matter where you're at, what your past was, what experience you have, it is just a learnt skill, it's about practice. Every one of us was born into the world and started at the same point, and our environment and life experiences and choices have led us to the point we are at today. Don't let your past dictate your future; your choices today can start you on the road to a bright new future. Everything you do in life, in your jobs and so on, was something you learnt, something you were taught. Lease options or any of the other No Money Down strategies are no different, they are just learnt skills. There are four essential rules to success:

- **Believe you can buy everything!**
  Believe you can buy absolutely everything. Why not? When money is no longer the problem, you can stop looking at cheap little properties and believe you can buy everything. Two of the people who attended my No Money Down training (Graham Page and Rachel Malugu) had no previous property experience, and a couple of months after the training they drove around the Yeovil area viewing million-pound-plus houses one Sunday morning. They rang the intercoms of the gated addresses of every house they saw with a 'for sale' board outside. Most of the people in the houses ignored the buzzer, some answered and told them they were not interested and one couple asked them to come back in an hour, so they went away and had a cup of coffee and then returned an hour later. This is the deal they agreed:

Case study: Graham Page and Rachel Malugu

Deal details:

1. Length of sales contract agreed (years): 2

2. Market value: £1.3M

3. Agreed sale option value: £1.0 M

4. Option consideration to buy: £1

5. Legal costs: £700

6. Total cost: £701

Exit options

1. Assignable contract sale profit: £299,299

2. 4% deal sourcing fee as BMV: £40,000

3. Purchase with vendor finance

The following are Graham's words:

This deal was a 10,000ft 6-bed, 4-bathroom house with swimming pool, on four acres of land, fully enclosed. The property was on the market with the estate agency at £1.3M but had not been moving (on for nine months).

We pressed the security buzzer on the gate in the outside wall and spoke to the vendor about how we were down from London looking for a property in the area and asked if we could view it. We were told to come back an hour later, which we did. After a tour of the property, which took about 90 minutes (understanding the vendor's situation, building rapport, etc. – he had actually built the property himself), we sat down for coffee with him and his wife. We had already found out that they'd only had two viewings in the last four months and no offers.

We discussed their future plans and asked whether they had a mortgage (including how long was left and the amount remaining). They explained that although they were not in a rush to sell and did not have a mortgage, they needed £1M to finance his next project in about two years' time – he worked in a builder's office dealing with commercial builds – and they would move into another house they owned up the road.

Our reason for questioning the vendor was to work out how we could help them achieve the best possible outcome for them by identifying the best win-win solution for all parties involved.

Upon mentioning commercial builds, light bulbs went off in our heads, so when we mentioned that we wanted to buy the property in the future, the vendor automatically knew we were talking about a sale or lease option, as he had dealt with these as part of his commercial build experience.

After further discussion, we agreed a sale option to buy the property within two years at an option price of £1.0M – he even added a clause that we could hand control of the property back to them at any time in the two-year period (not that we intend to do so – you should never enter a sale option deal if you do not mean to complete on the purchase).

We shook hands and sent the documents to our solicitors to be formally drawn up, agreeing to pay for their legal fees.

In terms of exit planning we have several options:

- Directly find an alternative buyer and sell on as an assignable exchange at £1.3M (potential profit £299,299)

- Move the property on as a BMV sourcing deal (approx. £40K profit)

- Purchase the property though vendor finance (if the vendor does not need the money for the project!), saving £250 in deposit money

- Purchase the property with a BTL mortgage and use it for serviced accommodation for celebrities or local businessmen and their families (estimated cash flow = £30k per month)

Note: The 'we' is my joint venture business partner Rachel and me – we met at the No Money Down Mastermind programme run by Kevin McDonnell. This provides a fantastic active support group who help each other to move forward with achieving and exceeding their property targets. We wouldn't have been able to achieve these results without the group and Kevin. If we hadn't attended the NMD, course we would never have dreamed of attempting to secure a £1.3M house, nor know how to go about it – we now have the mindset of 'we can buy anything!'

If you would like to do these types of deals, then why not go get them? There is no reason why you can't, all it takes is for you to get in your car on a Sunday morning and ring some intercoms. If you put yourself out there, you'll get the results; it's not about luck, you make your own luck. Don't let lack of funds stop you, money is not the problem! Money has never been the problem. There is more money in the world today than there ever has been. They're printing the damned stuff. There's enough money on the planet right now to make every single person in the world, not just this country, every person on this planet a millionaire. If you're not currently a millionaire, then who's got your cash? Seriously! Somebody has got your money. I spent years making excuses that I couldn't be successful as I didn't have the money to get started, but the truth is money was never the problem, and lack of money is not holding you back either. Knowledge is the problem; money is not powerful, knowledge is powerful.

1. Learn to market yourself!

Marketing is a fundamental key to success. I regularly speak to people who say they can't find the deals; I even saw one person posting on Facebook asking if lease options were done in his areas, as he never sees any advertised. Lease option deals won't be advertised in estate agency windows, you must market yourself as the local property problem solver and the deals will come to you. You need to be telling people what you do. The most successful people in any industry are putting themselves out there, marketing themselves. Nobody is going to come to your door and offer you deals, you have got to market yourself. You've got to put yourself out there and let people know what you do. For example, if a vendor is in negative equity, you won't see their house advertised via a high street estate agency as they will have to put their hands in an already empty pocket to pay the agents' fees – this is just not affordable for them, so they get stuck. I don't want you to think that lease options only work when people are in negative equity, as this is just one of numerous reasons why people would agree to a lease option. I'll share a list of some of the reasons later in this chapter.

2. You must build your network.

The most successful people I know are the ones with the biggest network of contacts. You can't do property on your own; it's no different to anything else in life, you need support to achieve great success. If you are looking to raise funds, or source and sell deals, you need a database of investors. It doesn't have to be a large database; 250 contacts would be a great target to start.

Attend networking events locally and nationally and have a target to speak to and get the contact details of as many people as possible. Now I know this comes very easily to some people, but it can be the scariest thing in the world for others. In my first 10 years in property, I attended about three or four networking events in total, and when I did go I was too afraid to talk to people. I guess in hindsight I was afraid that they would ask me how I was getting on in property and at the time it was very bad, everything I had tried had gone wrong. I also had the mentality that I was attending just to listen to the speaker, even though it was called a "networking event" – the hint is in the name. I now host two different networking events per month as I've realised the power of networking and education. There is an African proverb: "If you want to go fast, go alone. If you want to go far, go together".

Set a plan for what events you are going to attend and when, I suggest a minimum of two events a month, one of which is property-related and one business-related. Aim to collect at least 10-15 business cards per event if it's a two-hour evening event, and you should be targeting the entire room on full-day and weekend events. The biggest mistake I see people making when networking is to spend too long talking to one or two people and never get a chance to meet other people; maybe the most important person in the room is the one you didn't even get to meet. If you focus on collecting contact details, you can spend the rest of your life building the relationships with people, but if you go home without their details they may be lost to you forever.

Build your contacts, build your network, you control your future! I wasted 10 years before I realised the power of networking. Don't waste 10 years, start today. There are more than 7 billion people in the world. Each of us is just a speck on the planet; we will come and go quicker than you can imagine. None of us know how long we have here to leave a mark, so live your life to its highest potential while you're here. Do what you can to leave a legacy for your family. I spent 10 years making excuses;

leave the excuses behind. You can't change the past, but you can decide right now, today, what your future's going to be. Are there people in your list of contacts who can answer the phone to you late at night and help you with property? Who can speak to you and guide you by giving you the right advice? Who can help you move forward with your life? Or have you got people in your list of contacts who, when you tell them you want to do something positive, say "don't be stupid, you can't do that!"? Who are the people you have on your list? Because maybe you need to change them and get the right kinds of people around you – people who can help guide and support you to make a positive change in your life. I'm not saying I know the answer to everything – I absolutely do not and never will, we are all learning all the time – but what I do know is that if there's something I can't solve, there are people I know who either have the answer or know who does. To be successful you need to have access to likeminded, positive people who will support you and drive you to success.

3. You need a strong reason why

Why do you want success? Why are you reading this book? Why do you REALLY want to change your life? Write down your reason why – take a moment and write something down right now. Write down the one main reason why you want to be financially free. Really think about this, as it's not the money and it's not the property. Look past the property and the money, what's the money for? What's the real reason you want the money?

Is it that you want to have the fast car?
Is it that you want to leave a legacy for your kids, for generations to come?
Is it that you want to take care of your parents in later life?
Is it that you want to put your kids through private school?

What's that one reason? Write it down. Because if you don't know what your reason is, then it's likely you won't have the motivation and determination to keep going when things get tough. The reality is there will be bad days, things will go wrong; property is not easy, but it is most definitely the easiest hard work you will ever do. As Rob Moore says, "you have to work hard enough not to have to work hard" and this is so true of property. It's a simple process but it's just that little bit too hard for most people to bother trying. I spent a few months living how most people won't, so I can now live the rest of my life how most people can't – you can too if you just commit to getting the right education, putting in some time (five to eight hours per week) and taking action.

A lease option is one of the most powerful strategies in property today. It's not new, it has been around for about 100 years and yet it's a strategy that many people have never heard of – and those who have heard of it don't always fully understand how to use it effectively. Lease options have historically been more widely used in commercial property than residential property, but the concept is the same.

One of the biggest benefits of a lease option as a strategy is that it works where you are, it works in your area; it works everywhere, if you work. One of the main reasons people get into property is to get out of their jobs, but then they travel three or four hours across the country to find investment properties in an area they don't know very well. What they are doing is creating a second job, spending their lives researching a new area, which can take years to get right, and living in their cars on motorways. I want you to get out of your job, not create a second one. With lease options you can build your property business right on your own doorstep, no matter what part of the country you live in.

What is a lease option?

Lease options first originated in America and are also commonly used in Australia. The term 'lease option' is actually an American term, meaning a lease of a building with an option to buy it later (lease with option to buy). In America, tenants take out leases on residential properties, but in the UK tenants don't have 'leases', they have assured shorthold tenancy agreements (ASTs). The contract is still referred to as a lease option in the UK, although when your solicitor draws up the option agreement on a property it is not actually a lease option, it is a 'rental agreement with an option to buy'.

People also often confuse 'lease option' with 'leasehold' but they are completely different. 'Leasehold' is a type of property ownership in England and Wales which is most common with blocks of flats, although some houses can also be leasehold. With leasehold, a freeholder owns the land that the property sits on and the leaseholder owns the rights to part of the building for a specified period of time; the leaseholder doesn't have any ownership rights to the land the property sits on or to the communal areas if the property is in a block of flats.

A lease option is different: in simple terms, it is the right to buy something but not the obligation to buy it. You assume control of the asset and have the right to buy it, but you're not obligated to buy. You can give it back later if you choose or sell it on to someone else. If you take the example of purchasing land subject to planning permission, when developers buy a piece of land they usually agree a purchase price subject to planning permission being granted; if the planning gets approved, they exercise their option to buy the land, and if it doesn't get approved, they don't buy the land. They have used an option to give them control of the land and secure a purchase price so that they can reduce their risk while applying for the planning permission. This is known as a 'purchase option'. The good news is you can use the very same principles to control residential property, land or commercial buildings – options can be used on anything.

Options are not just used in property, they are used in various different industries and professions. Professional football teams use options to secure the purchase of footballers, for example. Liverpool agreed an option to buy Naby Kieta from RB Leipzig in the summer of 2017 with the player moving to Liverpool in the summer of 2018 and the price dependant on the position in which Leipzig finished in the German Bundesliga – the higher they finished the more expensive the price. In the same summer, Paris St Germain signed French forward Kyliann Mbappe on a season-long loan from Monaco with an option to buy at the end of season for £165.7M.

If you've got a car on lease, that's a lease option. You pay a small initial upfront sum to get control of the car, then you make a monthly payment to keep the car, and then you have the choice or option either to make a final balloon payment at the end to buy the car outright, or to give it back. It's the same process with a house: you pay a small initial upfront payment which can be as little as £1, then you make a monthly payment (the mortgage amount) and then a final payment when you exercise your option to buy (the outstanding mortgage balance). The only difference between buying a house today and taking it on as an option to buy later is the contract, everything else is the same. You still have mortgage payments, maintenance, insurance, tenants, etc., the only difference is you have taken control of someone else's title deeds instead of owning your own. It's called an option agreement – it gives you the right to buy the property at some point in the future. It's an option agreement that gives you control of the title deed, which gives you control of the house, which allows you to make the CASH.

Options are not new, they are used every day across many different industries, and you can use them to control property.

The benefits of using an option to buy over purchasing today

- No need to pay stamp duty: Stamp duty is payable on 'substantial completion' and as you only have an option to buy and are not exchanging contracts, then there is no requirement to pay stamp duty. Substantial completion generally occurs after exchange and receipt of keys; I will cover this in detail in chapter 8: Exchange with Delayed Completion.

- Reduced risk: Let's be honest, buying an investment property can be risky. When you buy a house in the traditional way, you must put down a 20-25% deposit and take out a mortgage, plus there are all the additional costs like stamp duty. That's a lot of money tied up in one deal. What if you get the area wrong? What if you get the price wrong? What if you can't find tenants or if it doesn't rent for as much as you had anticipated? With a lease option you get to 'try before you buy' – just like a sofa from DFS. This significantly reduces your risk: you can purchase it later if you want, you can sell it to somebody else if you want. You basically have control over the asset. If you're buying a property and you put £50K, £60K, £100K, £200K of your life savings into it, that's risky. Why not just control it? See if you can get it rented out, confirm that you could make a profit, and then buy it at some point in the future. Plus, and here's the best bit, you can buy it with the cash you make from the rental income from the house, so you're not using your own money.

- You don't need a mortgage: Being able to qualify for a mortgage is not the most important thing in property; knowledge is more important. You don't need to take out your own mortgage to make a profit from property, you can control someone else's mortgage. With a lease option, you assume control of the vendor's existing mortgage and babysit it for them, making the monthly mortgage payments on their behalf, and cash flow the property by renting it out to tenants for market rent.

- You don't need a deposit to get started: When I say no deposit needed, there is in fact a small deposit needed, which can be as little as £1. Just £1 can get you control of a property; you're not buying the property for £1, you are assuming control of the debt for £1. For example, if there is a property with a market value of £100,000 and if has an outstanding mortgage of £98,000 then there is a debt of £98,000 and equity of £2,000. You assume control of the £98,000 debt in exchange for a sum of money between £1 and £2,000. These types of deals are easily negotiated for £1, as it is much more than the seller would make if they sold it in the traditional way – even if they got the market value of £100,000, they would then have to pay agents' fees and solicitors' fees, which would eat up their £2,000 equity and then some, meaning they would have to put their hands in their already empty pockets to move on.

- You can help people in difficult situations: people need to sell their properties for various reasons, and quite often they are forced to sell on the cheap because the best offers they get are 75% BMV from investors. With lease options, you can offer them their asking price or even more, as it's not the price that's important but the terms of the deal. There are lots of different scenarios for when people might need to sell quickly, such as:

  - Moving abroad

  - Needs a refurb and nobody has offered

  - Relocation

  - Job move

  - Early redemption charge

  - No/negative equity

  - Avoiding repossession

  - Unemployment

  - Rising personal debt

Let's look at one scenario (there are hundreds): people who are facing repossession. There are people's homes being repossessed all over the country every single week of the year; when this happens, the bank takes the house off them, sells it under value and then chases them for years afterwards for the remaining debt, in many cases forcing people into bankruptcy, leaving them with bad credit for years to come. Using lease options, you can help these people take control of their property, babysit their mortgage for them, rent the property out and complete the purchase at some point in the future. They get to move on with their lives and avoid bankruptcy, so don't get scarred with its stigma. So why don't they just rent the house out themselves and avoid bankruptcy? The answer is simply that most people don't think like us – the thought of renting their houses out never even crosses their minds. They do not have the entrepreneur mindset. Don't make the mistake of thinking that everyone thinks like you, because the reality is that they don't, you are unique. One of the main reasons most people either don't get started in property or start but quit too soon is that they falsely believe that everybody thinks the same as them, and they can't get past their own thought processes. You've got to leave your shoes and step into the other person's to see life from their viewpoint.

You can make some serious money using lease options – serious money by focussing on owning nothing and controlling everything. Over 150 years ago, John D Rockefeller, widely considered the wealthiest American of all time, said: "The secret to success is to own nothing, but control everything". He was one of the most powerful men in America, and has left a lasting legacy that can be still seen today in iconic institutions such as The Rockefeller University and The Rockefeller Foundation – success leaves clues. If you want to build a lasting legacy for your family for generations to come, you need to be using No Money Down Investing techniques, as you will never be able to scale your business quickly enough using your own money. If you look at the richest people on this planet, they follow the Rockefeller principle – people like Donald Trump, love him or hate him. Trump follows the 'own nothing, control everything' principle. Whatever your thoughts are about Donald Trump, one thing that cannot be denied is that he has made himself the most powerful man in America, possibly the most powerful man in the world, and it all started with property and the use of options.

The lease option is one of the most powerful property investment strategies in the world, and it can make you some serious cash. The thing about cash is it doesn't make you a better person or a worse person; money makes you more of what you are. If you're already a horrible person, then money will make you a more horrible person. If you're already a good person, then money will make you a better person. Money magnifies what you are!

What about Uber? Uber is the largest taxi provider in the world, yet they don't own a single cab! How about Airbnb? They are now the largest accommodation provider in the world, yet they don't own any accommodation! The wealthiest people and businesses on earth focus on control – they follow the Rockefeller principle, 'own nothing, control everything'.

Follow a proven system and success will follow. I didn't create this stuff. I didn't wake up one night and say, "oh my god, I've just had a brainwave. Let's do lease options!" No, I just learnt these strategies. I just followed a system that was already there and became the best at it. It has completely changed my life, and it can do the exact same thing for you. You've got to stop thinking that you need to have deposits to buy property and start thinking outside of the box. Start thinking like a professional property investor. It's about knowledge! It's about control!

Why would anyone agree to a lease option?

Why would a vendor give you their house on an option to buy? Why not just sell it themselves? Why not just rent it out themselves?

Maybe they're unable to sell. Maybe they've tried to sell it for a long time and there have been no offers, or the offers were too low. Maybe they're relocating, moving elsewhere. Maybe it's because of a job move. There are literally hundreds or reasons why people would agree to a lease option. For example, I regularly speak to homeowners who have been given a relocation package by their companies due to a job move – they often need to move quickly to other parts of the country and around the world and they don't have time to sell the property before they need to leave. They are not landlords and don't want the hassle of managing tenants or dealing with letting agents, they've watched TV programmes like "Tenants from Hell". They've tried to sell the house without success and suddenly they're at the point at which they're going to be paying two mortgages. They just want to move on knowing that their home is sold and looked after. A lease option is often the perfect solution for them, as they get close to or equal to their asking price and they get their mortgage costs covered immediately with the purchase completed at a point in the future.

Remember, don't think everybody thinks like you. You need to be marketing and then fishing out the perfect type of person whose situation may mean they are open to an option agreement. I read a post by someone in a Facebook community a few weeks ago who said, "I've heard about lots of people doing lease option deals, but I've had a look and there don't seem to be any of those around Bournemouth." Right? So, as I've said already, you don't find lease option deals advertised in an estate agency window. You will not see a sign saying 'lease option deal available for sale' there. If somebody has a £100,000 mortgage on a property valued at £100,000, they can't afford to go to the estate agency because it will cost them money to sell the house – money that they might not necessarily have. There are other ways to find these deals. We use specific marketing to target lease option deals. I will cover marketing in chapter 6.

Maybe it's an early redemption charge. Many people agree to long-term fixed-rate mortgage products when they take out a new mortgage, then their circumstances change and they decide they want to sell their property, but selling during the fixed period means they get hit with early redemption penalties by their lenders, which can be anything from 1%-7% of their outstanding mortgage balance. Let's say you're speaking to the vendor who is looking to sell their home and they tell you that they have four years remaining on their fixed-rate mortgage. If they sell today, they have to pay a 4% early redemption penalty – selling their house today could cost them an additional £16,000 on a £400,000 house, that's a lot of money! Focus on solving their problem, saving them money, and you will automatically make money.

So why not propose an option to buy in which you exercise the option to buy after the fixed-rate mortgage period comes to an end, therefore saving the vendor from having to pay any early redemption penalty to their lender? Instead of trying to make an offer on the house to buy it today, show them how you can make them more money by not selling for a certain number of years – in this case four. You take control of the property today with an option to buy, babysit the mortgage for four years and then at the point at which the fixed-rate period comes to an end, you exercise your option to buy. As the agreement is put in place today, you babysit the mortgage, becoming responsible for all the payments, all the maintenance, everything! And in exchange, they get to move on with their lives, start the new job, etc., and not have to worry about the property, knowing the sale is agreed. Why don't you do that instead? It's a much easier negotiation when you're offering someone market value for their property than it is when you're offering 25% below market value (BMV). I spent 10 years walking into £100,000 houses trying to buy them for £75,000 – 25% BMV – and getting nowhere. Once I started to focus on the vendor and on how I could make them more money, I automatically started to make more money myself.

It is much smarter to focus on the sellers instead of what you want out of a deal. Find out the value of the property and how much debt they have on it, then offer them their equity in exchange for you taking over the payments on the debt. You then babysit their mortgage and, here's the best part, you will generally get better mortgage terms on the property by babysitting the current mortgage than you ever would taking out your own. AND you don't have to come up with a 25% deposit or pay stamp duty.

Do you always pay market value?

No, not always; you should always aim to negotiate the price, but you don't have to go as low as 25% BMV to get a great deal. With a lease option, it's never about the price, it's always about the TERMS, i.e. how long you will have the option for and what you agree to take responsibility for during the option period.

For example, a vendor has a property valued at £100,000 and they are trying to sell it for £100,000. On your fact-finding visit with them, they inform you that they currently have an outstanding mortgage balance of £96,000. This means if they sell the house for their asking price, they will get £4,000 equity. However, I wouldn't offer them £4,000 to walk away and let me take over the mortgage, because if they were to sell that £100,000 house in a normal sale via an estate agency, would they get £100,000 for it? Very unlikely! What would they get? Maybe about £97,000, as everyone wants a bit of a discount. Now they have £1,000 left and they still have to pay approximately £2,000 agency fees and £1,000 solicitors' fees. When you take all their fees into account, it will actually cost them money to sell the house – they will likely have to put their hands in an already empty pocket to pay money to get rid of the property.

Most people don't have any saving so cannot afford to sell as they can't come up with the money they need to walk away, they can't magic it up out of thin air. So I offer them £1 for the property. It's not really £1 for a house, it's £1 in exchange for a mortgage debt (in this scenario, you would be paying £1 in exchange for a £96,000 debt). Does that make sense? £1 for a debt. What this £1 offer has done in reality is saved them a few thousand pounds in fees, it allows them to move on with their lives and relieves them of all the stress and pressure they were under worrying about the property. Can you see how it saved them a few thousand pounds, because they didn't have to pay the estate agent's costs? Note: never cut an agent out of a deal if they introduce you, always pay them and pay them well, as they will then find you more deals.

> *"Never worry about the price of a shovel*
> *when you're digging for gold"*
> *– Mark Dalton*

Lease options don't just work where there is little or no equity, they work in any scenario in which the homeowner needs to liquidise their equity today. However, if there is a lot of equity and the homeowner wants their money out now and isn't prepared to wait until a future date, then there are other No Money Down strategies to use to secure these deals – strategies such as vendor finance and assisted sales, which I will cover in later chapters.

If you commit to learning about options and using them in your property business, you will recognise that pretty much any property deal can be negotiated, essentially because the person selling the property has a problem or reason for selling, and you are the local property problem solver – solve their problem and you make the money. Lease options really are a unique opportunity to help people in difficult situations. I've given you a few examples of where they can work well but there are over a hundred different reasons why somebody would give you their property on an option agreement. We cover all of these scenarios in my No Money Down training, which is the only training course in the UK that I am aware of that covers every No Money Down investment strategy available today. If you are interested in the training, you can email me at kevin@kevinmcdonnell.co.uk.

The benefits to the vendor

For most people, selling or buying a property is an emotional decision, not a financial one. It's often only a financial decision for an investor. If you currently only focus on the price when looking at properties, then you are potentially missing out on many great option deals.

Focusing on the benefits to the vendor is the key to securing an option deal – no one will agree to a deal that only works for you and not for them. However, most people only focus on what's in it for themselves, and this ends up costing them a lot of deals and therefore a lot of money. You must listen very carefully to the vendor to understand their situation and then work out how you can structure the option deal to solve their problem. The starting point for every vendor is that they want their asking price. But remember, it's likely they'll only understand the traditional way of selling a house, so you must clearly explain to them the benefits of not selling their property today, but instead allowing you to secure it on an option and complete the purchase later.

So, what are the main benefits? There are numerous different benefits and it can be totally dependent on the vendor's situation, but some of the main benefits are:

- They get market value for their property

- They get their asking price for their property – this is not always the same as market value, they may want more of less than market value

- They get their mortgage paid

- They get peace of mind

- They can walk away with stress and pressure relieved

- There's no dealing with tenants. Remember most people don't want to or don't know how to deal with tenants. Now maybe your reading this book and thinking to yourself that you don't want to deal with tenants either. If that's you, then tenant buyers and the Rent2Own programme are for you; I'll be sharing all about tenant buyers later in the book.

There are three stages to an option deal.

Stage 1.

You need to find a motivated seller. We use different methods and there are very specific marketing approaches to find lease option deals, which I will cover in chapter 6: Marketing.

Stage 2.

Focus on creating a WIN-WIN solution. If you buy a property below market value, that is WIN-LOSE. If you pay too much, that's LOSE-WIN. If you agree today's market value, take over the property today and complete the purchase at some point in the future, that's WIN-WIN, as the vendor gets their asking price and you get control of the property and can cash flow it for a profit. I will discuss this in more detail in chapter 7: Negotiation.

Stage 3.

Exit. The thing I love most about options is the different ways to exit; in any investment you should always be looking at your exit strategy before you get in, and with options there are three key exit strategies:

- Hold long term and rent to tenants – purchase option

- Secure on an option and sell your option to buy to someone else – sale option

- Secure an option to buy and assign the option to a tenant buyer – sandwich option

Purchase options:

These are used to you negotiate an option to buy on a property that you want to keep long term in your own portfolio and rent out to tenants long term for a profit.

Sale options:

With a sale option, you agree a purchase price with a vendor and sign an assignable 'head of terms agreement' that gives you a certain period to find a buyer for the property. The vendor gets the agreed purchase price and you get anything over this price that you manage to sell the property for. I love sale options – you don't need to outlay any money so there's no risk, and if you don't find a buyer during the option period you either negotiate an extended option or you hand the property back. These are great for deals that don't quite fit your Buy2Hold strategy or are maybe out of your area.

Sandwich options:

These work great on properties that don't quiet stack up as a Buy2Hold, i.e. maybe the mortgage is £450 per month and the rent is £500 per month so there would be no profit left in the deal after paying management and maintenance fees. Instead, you secure it on an assignable option to buy and then put a tenant buyer in place who also has an option to buy but at a higher price to yours. They pay an upfront option consideration for the right to buy, they pay market rent plus a top-up. I will discuss tenant buyers in detail in chapter 5: Rent2Own.

Consent to let:

If you take on a property that has a Buy2Let mortgage on it, then this property has the right mortgage product to allow you to put tenants in the property. However, if you secure an option on a property that has a residential mortgage on it, then putting tenants in this property without the lender's consent would be mortgage fraud. Therefore, the vendor must apply to their lender for a consent to let before you could agree to the option deal if your plan was to rent the property out. A consent to let is the lender saying to the vendor that they are happy for the property to be rented to tenants under the current mortgage product. If it is a residential mortgage and the consent to let is not granted, then do not continue with the option to buy if you plan to rent the property out – this would be mortgage fraud for one, but also if the lender found out, there is a chance they could call in the mortgage immediately, meaning you would need to complete a purchase quickly for cash or lose the property.

Never agree to an option deal that does not make you a profit today; you wouldn't buy a property today that didn't make a profit, so you shouldn't secure an option on one either. Turnover is vanity, profit is sanity, cash flow is king.

Sale and rent back:

The vendor can never stay in the property after you agree an option to buy their property off them – if the vendor was to stay on as your tenant, that would be classed as sale and rent back (SARB). SARB is regulated by the Financial Conduct Authority (FCA) and you must be approved and listed on the financial services register, which can be found at Register.fca.org.uk.

Prior to regulation in 2010, unscrupulous companies were offering to buy homes from struggling homeowners and then rent them back to them at a reduced rent. However, most of the schemes were either unaffordable or unsuitable for the homeowners, and they were also unethical, as the rent back was on an assured shorthold tenancy agreement which was usually 6-12 months. In some cases, at the end of this period the rents were hiked up to make it totally unaffordable for the previous homeowner to stay on as a tenant, and they were then evicted. This unethical practice led to the current SARB regulations. Never promise a homeowner that they can stay on as a tenant for any period, as you need to get vacant possession when taking on an option deal where the seller is the resident in the property.

You couldn't buy a house today and rent it back to the seller, so you can't secure an option to buy on a property and immediately rent it back to the seller either. Every part of the process of securing a property on a purchase option to buy is the exact same as when you buy a house in the traditional way. The benefit of the purchase option is you don't have to put up a huge deposit today and apply for your own mortgage. Apart from this, everything else is the same: you need to get legal representation and carry out searches just like you would with a traditional purchase. All that is happening is that the word 'Buy' in Buy2Let is being replaced with 'Control'.

Who else uses options?

Options are a lot more widely used than you might think, some of the most high-profile examples are:

Furniture firm MFI – a business with hundreds of buildings and thousands of employees, once worth £1BN – was in takeover talks to be sold for £1.

Ken Bates bought Chelsea football club in 1982 for £1.

I used to work as a Quality Manager for one of the UK's largest construction firms, Laing O'Rourke, but when I joined them in May 2002, they were known as Ray O'Rourke and Son, and were a sub-contractor based out of

Grays in Essex. At the time, John Laing International, the largest construction company in the UK for over 100 years, was building the Cardiff Millennium Stadium and made massive losses, forcing them towards liquidation. Ray O' Rourke saw an opportunity to move from a medium-sized subcontractor to one of the largest main contractors in the UK overnight and agreed an option to buy John Laing International for £1, taking on the company's £87M debt and renaming it Laing O'Rourke. They went from a £250M a year business to a £5BN a year business within a couple of years. Then in the recession, Ray O'Rourke went on to use options to secure other businesses, such as Bison precast in Swadlincote, Derbyshire, which was rumoured to be for £0.98 because he wanted to beat the pound.

You could say I got lucky because I worked for Laing O'Rourke during this period so I saw this happen and learnt it; tens of thousands of people work for them and many who were there during these times are still there today. The difference is I took action: I went away and got educated, I learnt how to use options myself. I was fed up of working to make someone else rich when I wanted to build my own dreams. But the great news for you is this is a learnt skill and you can do it too, you are no different to me.

Options are happening around you in your towns, on your streets, day in, day out, but you don't see it. If you want to be very successful then you need to follow the successful – start doing what the Ken Bateses and Ray O'Rourkes of the world are doing. The richest people in this country are using options. If you want to build a large property empire then you need to be doing No Money Down Investing; if you don't, no matter how much you start with, you will eventually run out of money. You'll hit a roadblock. No Money Down investment techniques will keep you in the game.

So why £1? It's a symbolic proof of exchange – something must exchange hands to make it a legally binding contract. It doesn't have to be £1, it could be £10 or £20, it can be whatever you agree that works for you.

Dealing with the lender:

When doing a lease option deal, you have to make sure you get consent to let from the current mortgage provider if the property is not already on a Buy2Let mortgage product. If you do not get consent to let and you put a tenant or tenant buyer in the property, then you will be in breach of the vendor's mortgage terms and it's likely that the buildings insurance will no longer be valid in the event of the need to claim.

There are two ways to seek consent to let:

- Ask the vendor to call their lender and ask for consent to let

- Assume the authority to speak to the lender on the vendor's behalf. You can do this by getting the vendor to sign a letter of authority to allow you to represent them in discussions with the lender.

When is it best to assume authority? You can let the vendor speak directly to their lender, but it's always best for you to assume the authority to do this on their behalf so that you can not only control the conversation but also continue to get updates from the lender during the term of the option agreement.

There is some critical information that you must receive from the lender in order to do your due diligence on the deal:

- What product is mortgage on now?

  - Is it a fixed-rate product?

  - Is it standard variable rate (SVR)?

  - Is it a tracker mortgage?

- What is the current rate?

- When will the current product end if it's fixed or tracker and what will the rate then revert to?

- Is it an interest-only or a capital and repayment mortgage product?

- Can the vendor have consent to let?

- Are there any arrears?

- Are there any early redemption charges (ERC) if the vendor sold today?

- What is the length of mortgage product, i.e. how many years are left? (If the vendor took out a 25-year mortgage seven years ago, there would be 18 years remaining.)

Can you secure a lease option on any property?

Technically YES, but not everyone will accept a lease option deal, just like not everyone will accept a below market value sale. I have coached and mentored thousands of people and one of the biggest reasons they were unsuccessful before working with me is that they tried to force their ideas onto a seller, they tried to get the seller to sell the house in the way they wanted. But you can't fit a square peg in a round hole; trying to push the idea of a lease option onto someone who does not want to do a lease option, who does not have the problems that would warrant agreeing to a lease option deal is like trying to fix a leaking tap with nothing more than a hammer – you make the problem worse. This is why a professional property investor has more than one tool in his toolbox – you focus on the person's problem and then use the right tool to solve that problem. The lease option is just one of the No Money Down tools; throughout this book we will be looking at all the different No Money Down tools so you are equipped to deal with each seller's circumstances.

NOTE: In 2011, the Scottish Law Society ruled that solicitors should not use lease options due to their concerns that investors and/or tenant buyers may later decide not to take up their option to buy, leaving sellers stuck with their property and the buyer at risk of losing their invested money. Due to this ruling, lease options and tenant buyers, which I will be discussing in the next chapter, cannot be done in Scotland. Delayed completions, which we will cover in chapter 8, are a potential way to achieve a similar outcome to a lease option, only the seller is obligated to sell and the buyer obligated to buy. I recommend you seek legal advice from a solicitor experienced in the Scottish property legal system if considering entering into this type of agreement in Scotland.

Case study: Purchase option

The property was sourced direct to vendor through a direct mail campaign. The vendor had rented the property out for a few years but had recently had some tenants who didn't pay the rent and trashed the property. The vendor was tired of being a landlord and didn't want to put more money into refurbishing the property and run the risk of the next tenants trashing it again; he'd just had enough of being a landlord and wanted an easier life.

We agreed an option to buy for the outstanding mortgage balance of £62,000 anytime in the next five years and I paid £1 to secure the option to buy. I knew that a light refurbishment would get the property into a lettable condition and it would rent out for £495 per month. This would give me a £172.53 pcm profit after paying the mortgage, management and maintenance costs, and properties on this street in good condition were worth £80K, so there was good equity built in.

Homeowner:

- Outstanding mortgage balance: £62,000
- Value: £65,000
- Mortgage (pcm): £252.47
- Agreed option price (5 years): £62,000
- Option consideration to buy: £1

Profit:

- Agreed option price in five years: £62,000
- Value after refurbishment: £80,000
- Rental income (pcm): £495
- Mortgage (pcm): £252.47
- Management and maintenance (pcm): £70
- Profit (pcm): £172.53

Case study: Rent2Rent with option to buy

A lot of the deals we do are a slow burn. What I mean by that is that we often track them for months before finally agreeing a deal. This deal is one that initially went on the market for sale at offers over £80K, but the property was marketed as being in need of a refurbishment, and in my opinion it was overpriced. We had several projects on the go at the time, so I didn't arrange a viewing or approach the owner. Instead, I added it to my watch list and noticed a few months later that it was back on the market for £89K, newly decorated, with photos on Rightmove. But I still felt that this was slightly overpriced, and as the seller had money for a refurbishment, I assumed that he would not be motivated – a lesson for me and you is that you should never assume something and always seek to find out. A few more months passed, and I noticed the same property now on the market for rent at £475 pcm. At this point, my interest was piqued, as the owner had clearly wanted to sell but had changed their mind and decided to rent. This is a clear sign of a motivated seller, as a likely reason for this is that they are struggling to meet the mortgage payments plus bills on an empty property and need to find a tenant to cover the costs – this transpired to be the case.

I found the owner's residential address details via Land Registry. If you visit https://bit.ly/2K0BQRH and enter the property address, you can download the property Title Register for just £3 and this will give you the name and registered residential address of the property owner. Note: there are some dodgy websites that will charge you much more than £3 for the very same information, so be careful which site you are on – always make sure you are on an official Land Registry website.

Once I had the owner's details, I got in my car one evening after 6.30pm, drove to the owner's home and knocked on the front door. I introduced myself as a local property problem solver who was interested in the property he had marketed for sale and asked if it would be ok to arrange a meeting to discuss the property… or was now a bad time? Clearly motivated to sell, now was not a bad time! He invited me in and offered me a cup of coffee. We sat and chatted about the property, and it turns out it was a property he had purchased as an investment property a few years previously, but he'd had two sets of problem tenants, one set that didn't pay the rent and one set that damaged the property. On top of that, the builders he had in to carry out refurbishment works had overcharged him for the quality of the work that was carried out.

He owed £85K to his mortgage lender and had the property on the market for £89K, as this was what he needed to clear all his mortgage debt and selling costs and just walk away. He didn't want to have more tenants but had put it up for rent as he'd felt pushed into it as he was struggling to keep up with the payments while paying his own home mortgage. He was stressed out by it all and just wanted to walk away. As he was already resigned to having to place another tenant in the property but not wanting to, he almost bit my arm off when I explained to him that I was happy to give him £85K for the property if I would complete the purchase any time during the next 12 years and cover his legal costs (he also saved on agents' fees as it was a direct-to-vendor deal). I paid him £1 to walk away and immediately took over all his liabilities for the property, i.e. the mortgage and maintenance costs. I then spent £6,234 to convert the property to a 5-bed HMO (he had already spent £10K on a refurb so all that was left was fire door, smoke system and emergency lighting to ensure HMO compliance) – I didn't have the money for the refurb so I put it on a 0% interest credit card and paid it back within eight months from rental income, making it a None of my Money Down deal.

Now speed up the process and take five Rent2Rent deals each making £1K per month profit – that's £5k per month, so in six months you have £30K. You can start buying one of the five houses, and the next, and the next, allowing you to build your portfolio for FREE!

- £6,234 refurb + £1 option consideration plus £1,400 legal fees = total investment of £7,635

- £1001 pcm x 12 months = £12,012 pa income

- £12,012 divided by £7,635 = 157% ROCE and all money back out of the deal including legal costs within 7.63 months

I also have the option to buy for £85,000 anytime in the next 12 years. Rent2Rent is a brilliant strategy to replace your income and get free of your job, but the properties are not yours and if you only do Rent2Rent you will never build a long-term asset-based legacy. I aim to secure an option to buy on as many of our Rent2Rent properties as possible, and I suggest you do too. Why? Just think about the following:

The Rent2Rent deal is making £1001 pcm profit and initial setup money is back out by month eight. The purchase price agreed is £85K, so if you buy with a 25% deposit you need £21,250 plus let's say £5K fees = £26,250 to buy the property. Therefore, from month nine onwards, you save the £1001 every month and in 26.22 months you have saved £26,250, which you then use to buy the house. Rent2Rent to create the cash so you can use the cash as the deposit to buy the very asset you have been renting, making it a No(ne of your) Money Down deal and a house for FREE!

The background to the deal:

- November – property on the market for offers over £80K

- Took off market and refurbished by owner – £10K cost

- Feb – put back on the market for £89K... Didn't sell

- May – put up for rent at £475 pcm

The agreed deal:

- Agreed to cover mortgage of £454 pcm

- Option to buy for £85K in the next 12 years

- Paid £1 for the option to buy

- Converted property to 5-bed HMO

- Cost of refurb: £6,234

- Rental income (pcm): £1,820

- Mortgage + bills (pcm): £819

- Profit (pcm) £1,820 - £819 = £1,001 pcm

Case study: Kamila Wszolek

The following are Kamila's words:

People say you should tell everyone about what you're doing and that this will lead to business coming your way. I did what I was told and kept everyone updated on my property journey via different channels. One day, the owner of the CrossFit gym I had been going to for a year at that point approached me and asked whether I wanted to buy his flat.

My first thoughts were *no, not what I'm looking for, we've just bought four houses at once and it's way too much stress!* That was what I was thinking, but of course I didn't say that. I asked him for more details, timescales, etc. That's when he said he was due to be repossessed two weeks later! My head immediately screamed – lease option! In fact, it was the only way we could help him. He was in arrears of £3,000 and was unable to let the flat out to tenants due to its poor condition and having no money to maintain it.

After discussions, we agreed a 10-year lease option to pay the amount of mortgage he owed on the property (he was in negative equity), pay his legal fees and take on the option immediately. It would work as a Buy2Let, but I had been hearing about SA and wanted to try it. Even though I wasn't sure whether this property would work, I thought that having such low overheads would make it a pretty low-risk trial.

Once the property went live I couldn't believe the turnover we were achieving! To say this was a successful trial of SA would be an understatement. Once I got the property set up and working, I knew that I had found 'my thing'. I have attended Kevin's No Money Down and Rent2Rent courses, and since then I have successfully taken on and set up an additional nine Rent2Rents, with more in the pipeline as I continue to expand my portfolio.

Mortgage arrears:	£3,000
Solicitor fees (both parties):	£1,500
Refurb costs:	£3,000
Agreed purchase price in 10 years:	£71K
Value at the time of purchase:	£60K
Current Value (2018):	£75k
Mortgage (pcm):	£265
Rent as a Buy2Let:	£500 – net cash flow £150pcm
Profit as SA (pre-tax, pcm) approx.:	£1,000 +

Chapter 5: Rent2Own

Rent2Own, also known as Rent2Buy, is a strategy that you can use to help first-time buyers get on the property ladder or help current homeowners move up the property ladder. Due to rising house prices, most people must start off by buying a small apartment or 2-bed terraced house, not because it's their dream home but due to affordability. And then every few years, they move up the property ladder one step at a time to bigger and better properties. Every time they have to move, there are additional costs for legal fees and stamp duty, plus the property market has potentially increased, meaning they pay more for the bigger home than they would have paid had they been able to afford to purchase it years earlier.

Yet I would still consider these to be the lucky people, as most never get the opportunity to own their own home. The average age of a first-time buyer in the UK today is 37, and in London and the South East it's mid-50s. With Rent2Own, you have the opportunity to not just make money from property but also help people by giving them the opportunity to own their own home.

Rent2Own allows someone to move into one of your properties on a rental agreement with a separate option to buy the property on or before an agreed future date; the purchase price is agreed upfront, and on signing of the Rent2Own agreement they assume control of the property as a tenant buyer. You lock in your profit on day one and they get the benefit of having a property they can call a home – they can decorate and carry out improvements to the property to add value, and as the purchase price is agreed upfront and locked in, any increase in equity over and above the agreed purchase price is theirs to keep.

Rent2Own is perfect for anyone who wants to own their own home but can't at this moment in time due to their current circumstances. There are literally hundreds of reasons why someone might not be able to own a home, such as:

- They don't qualify for a mortgage

- They don't have enough money saved for the deposit

- They can afford a smaller home but want something bigger

- They have an expanding family and their current home is not big enough but they can't currently afford bigger

Why would an investor prefer a tenant buyer over a tenant?

There are many reasons why an investor would benefit from having a tenant buyer as opposed to a tenant. Some of the key benefits are that tenant buyers don't need to be managed, as they have a different mentality to a tenant – what I mean by this is that they see the property as their home, so you save on lettings fees as you don't need a letting agent to manage them. Another benefit is that they have a contract to purchase the property at some point in the future but they assume all rights to the property from day one so all maintenance costs are the responsibility of the tenant buyer. They will generally improve your house, not reduce the quality. Even if the boiler breaks, whatever repairs are needed, it is the tenant buyer's responsibility. The savings on management fees and maintenance alone are massive.

If you have ever had tenants who came up with excuses such as the following as to why they couldn't pay the rent, then maybe tenant buyers are for you, as it is generally hassle-free property investing:

- "I'm sure I've paid you, you must have lost it."

- "I don't have the rent money this month, I drank it."

- "I can't move out because the other place I applied for won't accept me because you were evicting me."

- "The tenants in the flat above keep stomping on the floor every night until midnight. I can't get any sleep." I said, "does it bother you?" They replied, "No, I usually finish playing my trumpet around the same time."

If you are an investor and you currently own a single let property that is not making you a profit, or the profit is very little, then placing a tenant buyer in the property can massively increase your monthly passive income.

Another scenario in which placing a tenant buyer in a property instead of a tenant is beneficial is when the property is out of your area, making it difficult to manage remotely.

There are a lot of areas of the country where the yield on single let properties is so low that it doesn't make it a viable property strategy, but with tenant buyers you can get HMO returns from a single let house, as the tenant buyer pays the market rent PLUS a top-up known as an option consideration that can be credited towards their deposit should they exercise their option to buy, but non-refundable should they choose not to buy.

So how does it work?

There are a few different ways that you can structure a tenant buyer deal and the three main ones that I will explain in this chapter are:

- You buy a house and place a tenant buyer in the property

- You lease option a house and place a tenant buyer in the property

- You structure a deal for another investor and you take a fee for setting it up

Let's look at the first one. You buy a house and place a tenant buyer in the property. Now I know this is all about No Money Down Investing but remember you could still buy a property using other people's money, and I will be showing you how to do this in chapter 13.

Let's say you buy a property for £100K and take out a 75% loan to value (LTV) mortgage for £75,000 at 5% interest (other amounts are available and rates change all the time – speak to a property specialist mortgage broker to get current available interest rates; the average interest rate over the past 50 years is about 6%, but I will use 5% in the example for ease of calculation). This would give you an interest-only mortgage payment of £312.50 per month. If the market rent for the property is £600 and you rented it as a single let, you would have the following costs (approximately):

- Management fee – 10% = £60

- Maintenance costs – 10% = £60

- Voids – one month per year = £600/12 months = £50 per month

Therefore your £600 per month rent less costs of £312.50 for mortgage, £60 management, £60 maintenance and £50 voids, leaves you with £117.50 profit per month.

Now take the same property and place a tenant buyer in the home. The tenant buyer will not need managing so no need for letting agents; they are responsible for their own maintenance and there will be no voids as they have a contract to buy. This saving alone is £170 per month, increasing your profit from £117.50 to £287.50, and this is just the rental portion. There is also then the monthly option consideration top-up. Let's say the tenant buyer has agreed to buy the house in five years' time for £120K. As you paid £100K for the property on day one, you have locked in your selling price profit of £20K (£120K-£100K). The tenant buyers must pay an upfront option consideration to secure the option to buy and I usually set this amount at 3-5% of the purchase price, so let's say 5% for this example. That means upfront the tenant buyer will pay £6K, which is credited from their £120K purchase if and when they exercise their option to buy.

My aim is to ensure that the tenant buyer has saved 10% of the purchase price during the term of the option to ensure they have a minimum 10% deposit saved for when they apply for a mortgage – over the past 50 years, you could always get at least a 90% mortgage on a residential home, therefore 10% of £120K is £12K. That's means if they have paid £6K upfront then they need to pay an additional £6K over the five years. The amount they must pay monthly as the top-up is therefore calculated by dividing £6K by the number of months, which in this example is 60 months (five years). £6K/60 months = £100 per month.

So, the tenant buyer pays £600 per month market rent plus an additional £100 top-up that is credited towards their purchase should they exercise their option to buy. This means you receive £700 per month, less mortgage of £312.50 = £387.50 per month cash flow from the very same property that was only making you £117.50 cash flow as a single let. That's a 329% increase in profit. You get to make far more money than a traditional single let Buy2Let investor but at the same time you help people get on the property ladder who would otherwise not be able to own a home. This is a true WIN-WIN and a real game changer for you as a property investor.

Now let's look at scenario two: You lease option a house and place a tenant buyer in the property. We've covered lease options in chapter 4, so I won't go into the detail of how a lease option works again here. What I will show you is how you can make a massive profit from a property that you don't even own by placing a tenant buyer in the property that you have secured an option to buy on from the homeowner.

There are two options relating to the same property. You secure an option to buy from the seller, assign your option to buy to a tenant buyer and sit in the middle – you are the meat in the sandwich. Who makes most of the money? You do! Why? Because the meat is where the money is. For example, you secure the option to buy a property from a vendor for £100K, and the property has an outstanding mortgage balance of £100K – i.e. no equity. You pay £1 for your option to buy and babysit the current owner's mortgage. You then get a tenant buyer to move into the property on a Rent2Buy contract. The tenant buyer agrees to buy the house for £120K. Your option to buy is £100K, so immediately on day one you lock in £20K profit, as your option to buy is £20K less than for your tenant buyer. The tenant buyer pays 5% upfront option consideration (£6K) meaning on day one you are in profit by £5,999 as your option consideration to secure the house was only £1.

The current vendor's monthly mortgage payments are £472 per month, which you agree to pay, and the market rent is £600 per month. The tenant buyer pays £600 per month rent PLUS £100 per month top-up towards the option consideration. Your profit is £600-£472 = £128 plus the £100 top up = £228 per month passive income.

Your total profit for the deal would be £20K uplift in value plus £128 per month from rental income x 60 months = £7,680, giving you a £27,680 profit from a deal you secured for £1. Just 36 of these deals would give you £1M profit.

A good rule of thumb with a sandwich option is to ensure that your option to buy is always one year more than the tenant buyer's option to buy; this is because a tenant buyer will often wait until the final few weeks of a contract to inform you that they are ready to buy the property, which means if you option to buy off the vendor was the same length as the tenant buyer's option to buy from you there wouldn't be enough time to complete the transaction because the contract term will have expired. If you always set the agreements up with an additional 12 months on your contract to buy with the vendor, then it gives you enough time to get the purchase completed by your tenant buyer and enough time to deal with any unforeseen delays. For example, if I was to agree an option to buy from a vendor any time in the next eight years, then the maximum option to buy I would give a tenant buyer would be seven years.

In scenario three, you structure a deal for another investor and take a fee for setting it up. How this works is you market to investors who are looking to sell a property either now or at some point in the future and show them how they can make a bigger profit by holding onto the property for three to five years – you place a tenant buyer in the property who pays market rent plus a top-up instead of selling the house today. You show the investor how they can benefit from increased rental income by no longer having to pay for management, maintenance and voids, and you assume the role of an agent, where you source the tenant buyers for them, do all the referencing and checks to ensure they get the right quality of buyer, organise the contract and you a fee for setting the deal up. You can take a fee from the landlord for finding the tenant buyer and structuring the deal, and also from the tenant buyer for sourcing them a property. The fee would typically be £1K-£3K from each person. If you structured one of these deals per month with a £1,500 fee from each person, that would give you an additional income of £3K per month for the rest of your life, simply by offering a service that's needed.

This works well with accidental landlords and tired landlords. Note that you could also do this for residential homeowners, however I recommend you only structure these deals for investors as they tend to have a better understanding of tenants and contracts than a homeowner would. If you're looking to secure a property from a homeowner, I recommend either purchasing the property upfront or securing it on a lease option so that you stay in the deal and ensure it runs smoothly through to completion of the option to buy in the future.

There are four points in time at which you make money from a Rent2Own property:

- You take a little bit of profit upfront. This is known as the upfront option consideration.

- You take a little bit of profit monthly. This is known as the monthly top-up, which is the option consideration that is taken in addition to the market rent

- You take the rest of the profit at the end.

- And finally, you get the profit from the market rent less the mortgage costs.

I will run through an example below, but before I do that, imagine you secured a property for £100K and agreed to sell it to a tenant buyer for £120K. Your uplift in value profit would be £120K - £100K = £20K

Your maximum uplift in value profit is £20K, and you can take this profit in the three places listed above, i.e. a little bit upfront, a bit monthly and the rest at the end. For example, if you took £6K upfront and £100 per month top-up (for £6K over 60 months) that would mean you would have £8K left to take at the end.

£6K upfront + £100 monthly for 60 months + £8K at the end = £20K total uplift in value profit.

The final part of your profit is the difference between the market rent and the mortgage costs. For example, if the market rent was £600 per month and the mortgage was £472 per month, then the monthly rental profit would be £600-472 = £128 x 60 months = £7,680, giving you the £27,680 total profit mentioned earlier in the chapter.

You need to make sure that the monthly rental amount is paid as a separate payment to the monthly top-up. If and when the tenant buyer decides to exercise their option to buy at some point in the future, then they will need to apply for a mortgage with a lender. The upfront option consideration and monthly top-ups will be credited to them to be used as their deposit, so they need to be able to clearly show the bank that they have paid the deposit and not just rent. If the monthly rental income and top-up money is all paid as one payment, then the bank will just see this as rent and not deposit money. The rent must therefore be paid into your property business bank account and the upfront option consideration and monthly top-up money must be paid either into your solicitor's account or a client account – you must be able to clearly distinguish this as deposit money.

When I teach my mentees on our training courses about Rent2Own, one of the things that I find people struggle with is understanding how the payment of the deposit works. If you have been collecting the deposit money via option considerations over a number of years and these payments have added up to 10% of the property purchase price, the bank will lend the tenant buyer the remaining 90%. You don't have to pay the tenant buyer back the 10% collected so they can show it as deposit and then give it back to you again; it is your money and all you have to do is prove that it has been paid.

For example, if you are selling a house today for £100K and the buyer needs to get a 90% loan from a mortgage lender and they put the remaining 10% into the deal as their deposit, do they physically get the £90K from the mortgage lender? No! Where does the £90K from the mortgage lender go to? The lender transfers it to the buyer's solicitor and the buyer transfers their £10K deposit to their solicitor. Their solicitor then pays the full £100K to the seller's solicitor (your solicitor, as you are the seller). Your solicitor then pays off the mortgage company, deducts their fee and pays you what's left. This is how a typical transaction works. Does their mortgage lender ask to see the £10K deposit money? No! The mortgage lender emails the buyer's solicitor and asks for confirmation that they are in receipt for the £10K deposit funds.

This is a typical transaction. Now, if you take the same property but the buyer is purchasing it via a Rent2Own contract, they have been paying the 10% deposit monthly for X number of years, then they apply for a mortgage for the remaining balance. When the lender asks the solicitor for confirmation that they are in receipt of the deposit funds, the solicitor can say "yes we can confirm our client is in receipt of the deposit funds". They don't finish the sentence saying they have been receiving Y pounds a month for X years. Deposit funds are passed from the buyer to the seller.

The benefit of a Rent2Own contract is that you can access and use those funds upfront and monthly, as it is your money! Remember it is non-refundable should the tenant buyer not exercise their option to buy, so either way it's your money to do with what you wish. This is a very complex strategy and not one I would recommend attempting to do without support from an expert, but if you can get a good understanding of this strategy it is life changing.

So how do you make any Rent2Own deal a No Money Down deal?

Some money is always needed for any property transaction – either money to cover a deposit to purchase, money to pay a vendor their equity so you can release them from the property and take over their mortgage, or legal costs and estate agency fees. So how do you cover these costs if you know you can find the deals and find the potential tenant buyers but don't have any funds to get started? You use the tenant buyers' upfront option consideration to cover your costs of acquiring the deal.

For example, if you have negotiated the purchase of a £100K house and need a £25K deposit to buy it, then you would look for a tenant buyer who has £25K funds available, wants to be a homeowner but doesn't qualify for a mortgage today due to reasons such as bad credit or not having lived in the country long enough. You set their upfront option consideration fee at £25K, use their money to buy the property in your name and give them an option to buy on an agreed future date for a higher price, e.g. £120K.

Or you secure a deal on an option in which you agree to pay, for example, £3K to the homeowner for their equity and you immediately move a tenant buyer into the property. They pay £6K option consideration, giving you the £3K you need to pay the homeowner plus enough to cover legal costs and give you some upfront profit.

Never ever allow a tenant buyer to move into a property without paying some money upfront as an option consideration. If someone has no money to pay upfront, then the likelihood is that they will never be in a position to buy the house, as they have not learnt to save. The type of tenant buyer you want is someone who has tried to save up for their home but just can't save enough; by having some savings they are proving to you that they are serious. In addition to this, the upfront option consideration is your insurance against them changing their minds and not buying the house – there is always a risk that a tenant buyer might stop paying rent or damage a property. You have the very same risk with a tenant, but if it happens with a tenant you generally lose money as you usually only have one month's rent as deposit to cover any damage and rent arrears. With a tenant buyer, you have thousands of pounds in non-refundable option consideration money and monthly top-up money, which mitigates your risk much more than having a standard Buy2Let property.

You do not need money to be successful in property; money is not power, money was never power. It always has been and always will be knowledge that is powerful. Focus on getting the right knowledge and learning from the best, and you will be able to structure pretty much any deal with none of your own money and make it profitable.

What is the benefit for the tenant buyer?

There are many reasons why a person will benefit from being a tenant buyer over just renting and saving to buy their home. All the time they are renting, they are spending dead money that they can't get back and the property market is increasing in value, pushing house prices further and further out of their reach. Not everyone wants to be a homeowner but there are millions of people in rental accommodation in the UK who would much rather be buying a house. By securing a property on a Rent2Own contract, they are locking in the purchase price; if house prices continue to increase, this becomes a benefit to them, as any value increase over the agreed purchase price is theirs.

I would guess that most people reading this book are reading it as they are interested in investing in property or investment and wealth creation in general and want to learn how to invest using creative strategies. For this reason, people often tend to focus more on the financial aspect of a deal, but there are various other reasons why a person would want to be a tenant buyer that are non-financial. You see, most tenant buyers enter into agreements based on an emotional rather than financial factors. Some of the main reasons why our tenant buyers agreed to deals were:

- They wanted to have somewhere they could call home

- Their previous two landlords had given them notice to leave and sold the property they considered their home

- They wanted to be close to family but couldn't afford to buy today

- They had a growing family and needed a bigger house with an extra bedroom and a garden

- They don't trust banks

- They wanted to 'try before they buy' as they weren't sure if they would be staying in the area due to their job but didn't want to rent, so they liked the idea of having the option to buy but not needing to buy right now

These are just some of the reasons why people have applied for a Rent2Own property from me; there are many more reasons as everyone's reason is slightly different. This is a unique opportunity to help people – because of the massive increase in the average age of a first-time buyer, most people can only dream about owning their own home, but with Rent2Buy you are giving them a chance they would not otherwise have to get on the property ladder The government tried to help people with the Help to Buy scheme, but people were still having to buy houses at over-inflated prices. Lots of developers are now offering their own Rent2Buy schemes in which they sell off most of their newbuild houses and then offer the remaining ones via Rent2Buy. With both of these schemes, people have to buy newbuild houses that are typically overpriced and with paper thin walls. You can set up a business to offer the very same Rent2Buy opportunity but with older properties, where the prices are not over-inflated and where the tenant buyer in many cases has the potential to add value via refurbishment.

It's at this point that some people reading this will be starting to realise just how many opportunities there are to make a massive amount of money from property using little or no funds. And then your mind starts asking *what about the tax*? You're right, you will have to pay tax, but the tax is only paid on profit! It amazes me that some people decide not to start a profitable business because they might have to pay tax and instead stay just over broke! Let's not get successful. Let's stay in our jobs. Let's not make any money because if we make some profit, we might have to pay tax. My aim is to pay £1M per year tax – if I'm doing that, then my profit will be significantly more.

By the way, if you make a lot of money, you can hire a really good property tax specialist who will make sure you don't pay much tax – when you are a business owner, there are lots of tax-deductible expenses you can claim to reduce your tax bill. I would advise you to get a very good property tax accountant to help you structure your business in a tax-efficient manner. If you're looking for a good accountant, send me a message either via social media or email, and I'll recommend a few who I know well within the industry who can help you.

The paperwork

The tenant buyer will enter into two separate and independent legal contracts:

1. The option to buy agreement, which gives them the right to buy the property but not the obligation to buy the property at the agreed price at any point during the term of the option contract. If they miss any top-up payments, then the option to buy agreement is terminated.

2. The tenancy agreement, which gives them the right to occupy and enjoy the property during the option term, provided the terms of both agreements are strictly adhered to. If they don't adhere to the terms of the tenancy agreement, then they can be evicted following the same procedures as you would evict any single let tenant.

Once they have entered into these agreements they will be legally bound by them. Therefore, you should always advise them to seek the advice and assistance of a legal representative.

Over 50% of tenant buyers tend to return the keys and not purchase

This might surprise a lot of people, but the reality is that most tenant buyers never end up buying the property! So why would they pay all that money and then not buy? Because their circumstances change. Not only that, most people don't think like an investor; you are reading this book because you think like an investor. I've had tenant buyers hand back the keys to properties because of a change in circumstances when they could have sold the house for more than they owed me and walked away with a profit, but they don't – they just hand the keys back, as it's the easier option and an emotional decision, not a financial decision.

A lot of investors decide not to do tenant buyers because their plan is to build a portfolio of properties to hold for rental income long term, and they see tenant buyers as a strategy that loses them their properties after a few years, which means they need to re-enter the market at a higher price to replace the lost asset. However, having analysed the return form my single let rental properties over my tenant buyer properties, the ones with tenant buyers out-perform the single let rentals every time. This is because of the cost savings of management, maintenance and voids during the period of the tenant buyers' option to buy, plus the fact that they often give the house back in a better condition than you gave it to them – in most cases they have added value through refurbishment.

So why would the tenant buyer not complete their option to buy? On average, people move home every five to seven years, and generally the length of a Rent2Buy contract is five to seven years. At the time they agree the option to buy, their intention is to have a family home and they don't want to be managed by a landlord or letting agent, but life changes. Some of the main reasons why people end up not buying are:

- Divorce or separation

- Job move

- Want a bigger house

- Moving abroad

- Want to be in the catchment area for a better school

- Health issues

- Job loss

There are many other individual reasons, but these are the main ones that we have experienced with our tenant buyers.

Although you are within your legal rights to spend the option consideration money and monthly top-up money, as it is non-refundable, I always recommend that you invest it securely into a high-interest savings account or ISA. This is because although it is non-refundable, there are times when you might want to give it back. Why might you want to give it back? Because sometimes it just the right thing to do! What I mean by this is that if a tenant buyer left a property with no notice and there were some repairs required, then I would not pay back the option consideration money. But if they had been in a property for a number of years, had looked after the property and were fully intent on buying the home but they could no longer afford the property due to something like the loss of a job or health issues, in my opinion the right thing to do would be to pay them back some or all of their option money. This is your choice and you don't have to, but I believe it's sometimes the right thing to do; remember, you can always place another tenant buyer in the property.

There have been occasions when I have not refunded any money back, when I have refunded some money back and when I have refunded all of the money back. You will know what the right thing to do is; don't be greedy and hold onto all the money when you know the right thing to do is refund some. Often people only think about the one deal, but you have got to look at the bigger picture – if you focus on helping other people then you will automatically make more money. I believe in the power of attraction and what you give away comes back to you in bigger quantities. If someone feels like you ripped them off, then they will tell others and it will affect your business, but if people get something from you that they weren't expecting, they will sing your praises to other people and help promote and grow your business.

However, don't pay back money when you know it's not the right thing to do. I had one tenant buyer who I gave a property in South Wales to a few years ago, and for the first year everything was going fine. Then they told me they were moving to London but asked if they could keep the house and rent it to a friend. Although my gut told me this was a bad idea and it was not part of the contract so I was in my legal right to cancel the agreement there and then, I gave them the benefit of the doubt and agreed. They moved a tenant in and everything seemed to be going well for the next year or so. Then one day I got a call of the tenant buyer saying that their tenant was moving out and they no longer wanted the house, so they wanted all their 'deposit money' back – I explained that it was not deposit money but was 'option consideration' money that could only be used as a deposit should they exercise their option to buy but was non-refundable should they choose not to buy. I said I would take a look at the property and make a decision. I drove the four-hour drive from my then home in Derbyshire on a Saturday morning and arrived at the house around midday. When I went to open the front door, I noticed it was unlocked; I entered the house and it was clear that the tenant had not looked after the property – a number of cosmetic repairs were required, plus the boiler wasn't working and the back door was damaged. The option consideration and monthly top-up was £4,030, but the repairs required to the property were of a similar amount. I told the tenant buyer that under the terms of the contract they were not entitled to the option consideration money back as it is non-refundable.

At this point they threatened me and said that they knew I did a lot of property education training and would come to my events and tell people I didn't pay them back. It would have been easy for me to pay them back at this point, but it would not have been the right thing to do so I chose to not pay them back. Never allow someone to bully or bribe you into doing what you feel is not the right thing to do – stand your ground and do what is right. Refund people some money when you know it's the right thing to do and don't when it's not. This is your business, your life, and your chance to make money when you have the right knowledge, so don't chase the money or be greedy but do always stick to your beliefs and make the decision that you feel is right for you and your family.

It's very important that the upfront option consideration money is called 'option consideration money' and never referred to as a deposit. If you refer to it as a deposit with a tenant buyer, then they will see it as a deposit; deposits are refundable and should either be lodged or insured against via a recognised government tenancy deposit scheme, option consideration money does not.

Even though over 50% of tenant buyers don't buy, never enter into an agreement with the intention of getting the house back. What I mean is never give a house to a tenant buyer you think will never be in a position to buy, always ensure you pick a person who is suitably qualified and in the best position to complete the purchase at some point in the future. I have never entered into a Rent2Buy contract thinking the person would never be in a position to buy. You should always get the tenant buyer applicant to supply you with a copy of their credit report and get them to speak to a mortgage broker to confirm that the broker feels if they were to make the monthly payments as agreed for the period of the contract they would be in a financial position to pass affordability checks with a lender in the future. You can never 100% guarantee this, but you can mitigate the risks as much as possible. Should anything change in their life that would mean they were not able to qualify for a mortgage during the agreed contract term, you could always extend the option period for them to give them enough time to qualify for a mortgage.

The great thing about Rent2Own is that you are in control and can help people improve their lives, and you get to feel like you have done something good for people and made money at the same time. Far too often, landlords are berated in the press and seen as stopping people from being able to get on the property ladder, but with the Rent2Own strategy you are doing the exact opposite – you are helping people get on and move up the property ladder.

Case study: Property secured on option and tenant buyer placed on contract to buy

Profit:	£115,000 - £85,000 = £30,000
	£3,100 taken as an upfront option consideration
	£100 per month top up x 84 months = £8,400 over 7 years
	£18,500 final payment at the end= £30,000
Plus, monthly rental profit of £450-£282.62 = £167.38 x 84 months = £14,059.92 from rental income	
Total Profit = £30,000 + £14,059.92 = £44,059.92 over 7 years That's a profit of £6,294.27 per year for a deal secured for £1,000 = 629% ROCE	

This deal was negotiated direct to vendor. I was driving the streets in my area one afternoon and noticed the front door open with someone in the hallway inside carrying out some repair work. I knocked on the front door and introduced myself to the person in the hallway, who happened to be the owner – he had purchased the property a few years earlier as an investment and had rented it out but he'd had some issues with tenants not paying the rent and damaging the property. He had planned to carry out some repairs and then put the property on the market to sell. After building some rapport, I gently asked him about the current debt on the property, which he said was £85K – he needed to sell for £90K to clear all his debts, as he needed money for legal costs, estate agents and the cost of the repairs he was carrying out.

According to my research, properties on that street in a good condition would sell for around the £100K mark, so I knew there was good potential to add some value. I explained that if he was to finish the refurb and sell via an agent, there was still no guarantee he would get the price he needed. I offered him £1K to walk away and leave the property as is – he could down tools and not have the work and emotional stress of having to prepare the house for sale and wait for a buyer. He would get £1K and I would take on the £85K mortgage debt and babysit his mortgage. He already had a family home so didn't need to apply for another mortgage, and there was no need for me to speak to the lenders as the property was already on a Buy2Let product.

Once the deal was secured, I placed a 'Rent2Buy' sign in the front garden and within a few days I had over 50 applications. I reviewed the applications and invited eight people to a block viewing. On the day of the viewing, I arrived early and parked down the street to see who would show up – it's always a good idea to let people show up at the property before you and start to mingle outside, as this builds desire and competition for the property before they even enter the house. I waited until five or six people were in front of the house and then I walked over, introduced myself and went to open the front door. Before I had even managed to get the key in the front door one couple said, "we want the house, how soon can we have it?" This kicked off a mini argument between two or three of the viewers, at which point I asked people to calm down and I would explain the process, which is as follows:

- The house is secured as is, they can refurbish to their standards and taste to make it a home and add value

- The first person to pay the option consideration of £3,100 gets the house

- They pay the market rent as normal plus a top up

- They have option to buy the house at any point during the next seven years

- Application is subject to credit check

- Once the credit check is passed, we complete all the paperwork and they get the keys to their new home

- Unsuccessful applications are placed on a waiting list for the next property

We continued into the house and before we had even gone upstairs the same couple came to me and said "ok, we will take it, we run a pub a couple of streets away and want a home nearby, this is perfect."

Within two weeks they had the keys to their new home and I had secured a profit of £44,059.92 over seven years without having to do any refurbishment or put any money into the deal. The £1K to the vendor was paid out of the £3,100 received form the tenant buyer.

A true WIN-WIN-WIN deal. The vendor won, as he got to walk away from a property that had caused him stress. I won, as I locked in my profit from day one with no need for management and maintenance costs. The tenant buyer won, as they got on the property ladder for a small initial deposit.

If you were to just secure two of these deals every year, from year seven onwards you would be completing the sale of two properties per year for the rest of your life. If you targeted a £44K profit per deal, that would an £88K per year income secured for life from just two deals a year! And this is just two deals per year from one strategy!

Agreed option deal with homeowner:

- Outstanding mortgage balance: £85,000
- Market value: £90,000
- Mortgage: £282.62
- Agreed option price (eight years): £85,000
- Option consideration to take on mortgage: £1,000

Tenant Buyer:

- Agreed option price (seven years): £115,000
- Upfront option consideration: £3,100
- Monthly rent: £450
- Monthly option consideration top-up: £100

Student case study: Yvette Mallinson
Property purchased and tenant buyer placed in the property on option to buy

The following are Yvette's words:

Our investment model works best when we find the perfect property for a tenant buyer based on their individual circumstances, i.e. their desired property type and location; monthly rent and purchase price budget; and the timeframe they need to qualify for a mortgage.

Jane responded to one of our Gumtree adverts for tenant buyers. Her situation was that her husband had sadly put the family into financial difficulty. By association, she had inherited significant debts and a poor credit rating. The relationship had broken down and Jane and the children had moved into rental accommodation. Unfortunately, they'd had to move three times in two years, owing to landlords wanting their properties back to sell. This was incredibly unsettling for the family.

Jane wanted to purchase a home, but she needed time to pay down her debts, repair her poor credit and save for her 10% deposit to qualify for a mortgage. She was in full-time employment with a good job working for the local government. She'd calculated her budget for purchasing, plus her monthly affordability for the rent and debt repayments (which once the debt was fully repaid in 12 months would then go towards her mortgage deposit). She required a 4-bedroom house close to her children's schools.

Once the brief was established, we found some potential properties on Rightmove, one of which was this ex-probate 4-bedroom Victorian terrace, which was structurally sound with beautiful character features, but in need of cosmetic refurbishment. Jane was thrilled by the prospect of a project and putting her own stamp on her home, in her own way, in her own timeframe and according to her own budget.

The property was on the market for £169,995 but we estimated it to be worth £160,000. Refurbished comparables were valued at £185,000-£190,000. Given the fact that Jane would be doing the work herself, we agreed a sale price of £189,000 in five years' time – a true win-win, given we had negotiated our purchase at £147,000 due to the vendor needing a quick sale, having found another property to buy. We fixed Jane's rent at £950pcm and she paid a non-refundable upfront deposit of £5,000 which meant she was motivated to see the transaction through.

The benefits for us are clear: a motivated tenant, no maintenance or management costs, no voids, plus an attractive return on our money. The combined upfront deposit, net cash flow and capital uplift produced an overall return of 153% over the term, or just over 30% pa. More than that, we'd helped Jane achieve her goal – no more uncertainty of a landlord selling up, the ability to improve her own home in her own way (plus benefit from any capital appreciation) and the ability to budget for the future. The reward of helping a family get back on their feet is ultimately priceless.

We have now completed five Rent2Own deals and have set goals to accelerate the acquisition process with Kevin's support in the next year.

- 4-bed mid terrace house in Hull (ex-probate, but habitable)

- Purchase price: £147,000 (market value £160,000 current condition, £185,000 good order)

- Money in: £44,750 (25% deposit plus purchase costs £8,000)

- Fixed rent: £950pcm

- Net cash flow: £625pcm (mortgage £275pcm, gas cert £10pcm, buildings insurance £40pcm)

- Agreed tenant buyer sale price: £184,000 (£189,000 less £5,000 upfront deposit)

- Option term: five years

- Profit:

Upfront option consideration: £5,000 (non-refundable)	
Net cashflow: £37,500 (£625 pcm x 60 months)	
Equity uplift: £26,000 (£184,000-£147,000-£11,000 purchase/mortgage fee/sale costs)	
TOTAL PROFIT: £68,500 ROI = 153% over term / 30.6% pa	

Do you currently rent? Why not Rent2Own?

If you are reading this book and you currently don't own your own home, or you do own your own home but have always dreamed of living in a nicer property, then the opportunity to do this is closer than you think. So far in this chapter I have discussed how you can help other people get on or up the property ladder, but what about you? Why not become a tenant buyer yourself?

The first three homes I lived in personally were all secured on Rent2Own contracts. Why? Because I couldn't afford to buy a home for myself due to my massive debts from losing money on Eastern European property investments and I didn't want to rent from another letting agent or landlord. But most importantly, it made more financial sense to Rent2Own rather than just rent.

If you follow the advice in this chapter, you could be living in your very own Rent2Own property within a few weeks. However, you don't want to be securing a Rent2Own deal from another investor, you want to be the person making the most money by securing the deal directly from a landlord or estate agent and then instead of putting a tenant in, you move in yourself in – you want to be the person securing the property at the lowest price possible and not the person taking it off an investor at the higher price. The great thing about this strategy is that a lot of the dream homes that you want to live in are the very homes that get stuck on the market and homeowners find difficult to sell. Why? For the very same reason you don't just buy it today: most people can't afford that type of property, so there are a very limited number of buyers. This means that you can easily agree to a creative purchase with the homeowner.

When I moved to the UK from Ireland in 2002 to work for Laing O'Rourke, I was offered a room in a company house until I "found my feet"; seven years later I was still in the same house having lived rent free all that time. Now this sounds great, but the problem was that I was young and I'd had no financial education. It was such an amazing opportunity to save and invest the money I was saving from not having to pay rent, but like 99% of people, I lived to my means – the wealthy delay gratification. Although I had no financial education, I mistakenly thought I had, and made that ill-fated decision to invest the little savings I had on deposits for the off-plan properties abroad, so by 2009 I was over £100K in personal loan and credit card debt taken out to cover the stage payments on properties that were worth nothing.

Then in 2009 I was asked to move to a new role in Nottinghamshire, and as the company accommodation was not part of my contract, I had to find my own place to live. Every spare penny I had was going towards servicing the debt and I couldn't afford to rent even a room, never mind a full house. I decided to find a property that I could rent and then let some of the rooms out to other people to help pay for the house. I looked for properties that were on the market to let and for sale. This is a great strategy for Rent2Own, as the vendor is telling us via their marketing that they are already open to the idea of renting their home and selling it at the same time. The reason a house usually has a 'for sale' and a 'to let' board outside it that the owners really want to sell but can't find a buyer, so they need to rent – every month the property is empty costs them money that they can't afford to pay.

I viewed a property one evening with a landlord who was looking to sell the house but had struggled to find a buyer so had placed the property on the market for rent although their preference was to sell. It was a 4-bed detached house with separate kitchen, dining room and sitting room. Her situation was that she had lived in the property for over 15 years and brought up her kids in the house with her ex-husband. She had been given the property as part of the divorce, but she was now remarried and had tried to sell the house previously but couldn't find a buyer. She had then rented it out, but the tenants had done what she considered to be damage (but in reality was nothing more than a few scratches on the walls, so this immediately indicated to me that she was not cut out to be a landlord as she was too emotionally connected to the property).

The house was on the market for £172,500 and available for rent for £700 per month. I had worked out that money wasn't the most important thing to her, the most important thing was that her home would be looked after, rent paid on time and a guaranteed sale in place. I offered her a £162,500 purchase price but on the basis that I would initially rent the house for £575 per month and then buy it later. The £162,500 offer was £10K less than the asking price, as I was expecting her to negotiate up, but when

I made the offer she immediately said "yes" – I almost replied back with "F**k! Why?" because in that moment I realised I could have secured it for less. You see, it wasn't about the money for her, it was an emotional decision!

We agreed that I would pay a £3,500 upfront option fee that would be deducted from the purchase price should I exercise my option to buy, leaving £159,000 (£162,500 - £3,000) to be paid at any point in the next 12 years to complete the purchase. I turned the dining room into a fifth bedroom, moved into one room myself and kept the smallest room as a little office, leaving three rooms to rent out. I spent £3,227 getting the property furnished and ready to move into myself and let the other rooms. That was a total cost of £3,500 + £3,227 = £6,727 – I put it on a credit card as I didn't have the money, but I knew long term I would save as I would get to live there for FREE. How? Well, these were the numbers:

- Agreed to rent at: £575 pcm

- Agreed option to buy at: £162,500 anytime in next 12 years

- Upfront option fee (deducted from purchase price): £3,500

- Furnishing and ready to let costs: £3,227

- Total investment: £6,727

- Bills (pcm): £367

- Total monthly costs: £942 (£575 rent + £367 bills)

- Rental income (pcm): 3 rooms x £325 = £975

£975 per month income, giving me a free bedroom and a free office, plus I'm up £33 per month – not a bad deal. I know it's not for everyone, as some of you reading this won't want to live in a shared house, but if you are currently renting a room then you need to be thinking about this as a strategy to get you on the property ladder.

Like anything, there are upsides and downsides to living in a shared house. You need to be able to get on with other people and if it's your own house you also need to be careful who you rent rooms to – you can get good tenants and bad tenants. I didn't properly check out the tenants that were moving in, and there was one particular tenant that springs to mind who was a complete nightmare. I used to come home from work in the evening, wanting to be able sit, watch TV and just relax, but this person would always want to sit and watch something different. I'd go to the kitchen to cook something and there they'd be, watching me cook. That wasn't too bad, but then I'd come home from work and they would be inside the front door welcoming me home; I'd come out of my room and they would be standing outside my door… anywhere I went in the house they seemed to be there, it was proper stalking! It got so bad in the end that they started coming into my room! At that point there was only one thing I could do, I had to marry her!

I met my wife in the house, and those of you who get to meet her (and I hope we do get to meet one day) will clearly see that she was the one stalking me and not the other way around. Wink wink. I'd better stop now, or my story will be that we met due to property and got divorced due to a book, LOL.

We lived together in the property for about another year and then decided we needed our own place, as it's difficult living in a shared house when you are a couple. I was still in massive debt and couldn't afford to move unless I did a similar sort of deal, so we agreed to wait until we found a property that we could Rent2Own. At this point, I was already starting to build my property business and was marketing for motivated sellers and tenants. A couple of months later, I rang a landlord looking for a reference for a tenant and while I was on the phone he asked me if I managed houses in the area – he lived 90 minutes away and wasn't happy with the service from his current agent. I said what I've learnt to always say, which was YES, and then I could think about it later. I viewed the property and it was in bad condition, needing new carpets and decorating, but it was a newbuild house only about seven years old, so I knew it could look lovely and be a great place to move into myself once it had been done up. I offered the landlord guaranteed rent with an option to buy, and he accepted the offer as he had bought it from a developer a few years earlier for a discount, and it was a hassle-free arrangement for him with a guaranteed profit locked in. The numbers we agreed were as follows:

- Agreed to rent at: £525 pcm

- Agreed option to buy at: £115,000 anytime in next nine years

- Upfront option fee (deducted from purchase price): £1

- Furnish and ready to let costs: £1,500

- Bills (pcm): £350

- Total monthly costs: £875

- *The landlord agreed to fit the new carpets, paint and decorate*

- Total investment: £1,501

We kept the first house and rented out the three vacant rooms (my room, the office room and Linda's room) at £400, £320 and £280 pcm = £1,000 pcm, saving us £175 pcm by moving! The first deal became a Rent2Rent, while still having the option to buy.

We then moved to a third house, a large 4-bed detached house on the edge of the Peak District, again on a Rent2Own contract. We kept house no.2 and the income from house no.1 and house no.2 paid for house no.3.

If you want to live for FREE, then focus on getting some Rent2Rent properties initially and use the income from these properties to pay for your dream home.

Chapter 6: Marketing

So how do you find the deals? The key to any successful business is marketing. Property investors or aspiring property investors often talk about their 'strategy' and mention things like single lets, HMOs, serviced accommodation, commercial conversions, etc. but I don't consider these 'strategies' – I see them as types of investments. What I mean is if you focus on HMOs as your strategy, for instance, does that mean you won't consider other types of deals if you find them? You see, once you start looking for deals, all types of opportunities start to appear.

Therefore, my primary strategy is MARKETING – I market for motivated sellers, I market for tenants and tenant buyers and I market ME to raise private investor funding and find joint venture partners. People need to know you exist; nobody is going to come knocking on your door offering you an opportunity, you need to go looking for the opportunity. It's "seek and you shall find", not "stay at home and tell nobody what you do and success will come to your door" (or, as the old Chinese proverb says, "Man wait long time with mouth open for roast duck to fly in").

I've tried lots and lots of different ways of marketing over the last few years; I've spent thousands of pounds on stuff that doesn't work and I've spent money on stuff that does work – I finetune that down to the stuff that works. In this chapter, I will share with you the marketing techniques that have worked best for me.

Focus on marketing to raise awareness of you, and let people in your area know that if they have a property problem, then you are the go-to local property professional to solve that problem for them. Then you focus on solving their problem, and if you can get a deal for little or none of your own money that makes you a profit today, do the deal. Prioritising marketing as my primary strategy has enabled me to build a £5M+ portfolio in just four years with a monthly positive cash flow of over £20K. A portfolio made up of single lets (flats, terraces houses, semi-detached houses, detached houses), HMOs, commercial conversions, a block of flats and land.

How can you position yourself as the go-to expert?

This might sound very simple, but you literally just claim the space! Market yourself more than the competition and you will automatically be seen as the go-to expert. There are literally hundreds of different ways to market yourself to different sectors, and different things work better for each type of investment, but you must ensure that you do a variety of different things to get your message out there – you cannot focus on just one method. Have you heard of seven points of contact? People need to know of you or hear from you at least seven times before they will begin to listen to you or trust in you, so if you're only focusing on one method of promoting yourself, it will be too slow, as you'll need to put the same message out there at least seven times. But if you have more than seven different messages, you can get the seven points of contact in just one day. I'm going to cover the four different clients you need to market to in order to grow a very successful business, and look at the top seven ways to target your audience.

The four different types of client you need to market to:

- Motivated sellers

- Tenants

- Tenant buyers

- Private finance and JV partners

Marketing for motivated sellers

What marketing methods can you use to let people know that you buy houses? How can you get your message out there so people know that you buy houses? What sorts of things could you possibly do? There is an absolutely endless number of things you can do to target motivated sellers; tell everyone what you do and place your message in as many places as

possible. Any idea you can think of that might work for marketing, test it! Marketing is the lifeblood of your business – if people don't what you do, then they won't know to ask you for help.

To get you started, here are our top seven tried and tested methods of finding motivated sellers:

1. Estate agents and letting agents

It might sound obvious, but it still surprises me just how many people don't build relationships with their estate agents and letting agents to get deals – they are spending money on marketing to target people who are looking to sell or rent their properties, and you can leverage this to find motivated seller deals. Yes, most deals in an agent's window are not motivated sellers, but I would suggest that there are always one or two deals on an agent's books at any given time where the seller is highly motivated either to sell or rent their property and open to a creative deal.

You don't necessarily need to do lots of deals with an agent to show them that you are a serious property investor who they would want to work with. There are other effective ways that you can quickly build credibility with an agent. One of these is to visit the agents regularly and get to know them; whatever you do, DO NOT go in, hand them a business card and introduce yourself as a 'professional property investor' – they get this all the time and they'll see you as a timewaster. I own my own letting agency and the staff always joke about the amateurs coming in trying to show themselves off as big gun investors, dressed in suits and ties and carrying fancy business cards, talking in big words but making no sense whatsoever. The serious investors show they are serious not by what they wear or what's written on their business card, but through their knowledge of property, knowing their numbers when it comes to house prices and rental prices, knowing tenant demand and tenant demographics, knowing which areas are good and which to avoid and understanding things like current market conditions.

You can build credibility before you ever visit an agency by giving them the perception that you are a company with staff. How can you do this? Use websites like PeoplePerHour. Go to www.peopleperhour.com and search for telemarketers – there are hundreds of people you can hire to make business calls for you. Hire one of them to ring all the agencies in your target area and give them a script that matches the type of deal you are targeting. For example, "Hi, I'm Lucy from xyz Property Company and we are currently looking for property in your area. Do you have any 3- or 4-bed properties on your books between X and Y price range that may be in need of refurbishment or that the vendor needs to sell quickly?"

Then get Lucy to send you a list of the properties that the agents recommended so you can do some research on them to see which may work for your strategy. Identify the properties that suit you best and then ring the agents back, saying "Hi, I'm Kevin from xyz Property Company, I believe you spoke to my colleague Lucy earlier. She told me you have this property that is of interest to us, could we arrange a viewing or can I arrange a good time to call into the office?" Now you are not just any property investor with a business card, now you have created the perception that you are the owner of a property company with staff.

Another way to build credibility and the perception that you are a bigger player than you are is to leaflet drop all the estate agencies' boards across your investment area once a month and make sure the agents know it's you by giving them the same number you put on the leaflets (they always check their system to see who is dropping the leaflets). When I tell people to do this they often panic and think we can't do that, it will upset the agents, but trust me, the agents target each other's houses with leaflet drops and door knocking all the time, so you distributing some leaflets is the last thing they are worried about. What this does is give them the perception that you are big player in the local property game now and have money to spend.

You see, they think you have dropped 50,000+ leaflets every month, but in reality you might have only dropped 50 leaflets; the cost of printing and distributing 50,000 leaflets is about £2,500, compared to £25 for 50, so immediately you have created a perception that you are a big player who they need to get to know and work with. After all, anyone with a £2,500-a-month budget for leafletting has got a lot of money to invest in property. One of the main reasons people struggle to get agents to work with them is when they need to provide proof of funds and they don't have them – if you do this one credibility-building strategy, you will often not even be asked for proof of funds upfront because you have created the perception that you have the money.

2. Leaflets

Have you heard that leaflets don't work? I have heard this many time and it's true – they don't work if you don't post them. They do work if you do post them, if you do it correctly. Like anything, there is a system to use for leafletting that will get you a much higher conversion that just blanket dropping across a town. I'll share the system with you in a few minutes, but first let's look at some of the biggest mistakes you can make when leafletting.

Right at the top of the mistakes list would be not leafletting either because you think it doesn't work or you took advice from someone else who thinks it doesn't work. If you walk into any small business in the UK, like a local takeaway, and ask them what brings in the majority of their business, they will immediately tell you it's leafletting – it's their bread and butter, and it should be yours too.

Not reviewing your leaflet before distributing copies is also a big mistake. I know of one property investor in the North East who designed, printed and distributed over 10,000 leaflets and then waited for a call but the phone never rang; he asked a fellow property investor to review the leaflet and see how it could be improved, and they noticed that he had left one digit of his phone number off the leaflet – no wonder the phone didn't ring!

Another rookie mistake is putting your website details on your leaflets. This is one of the biggest mistakes I see people making – they think they need a website so they can put the address on all their marketing materials, creating the perception that they are a big company. But putting your website details on a leaflet will dramatically reduce your response rate. Here's why: if someone gets a leaflet and it has a phone number on it and a website address on it, will they ring you immediately or Google you? 99% of the time they will Google you to find out a bit about you before ringing. However, the problem is they won't type your full website address into the search engine, they will only type part of it. Try this now and see what happens. Let's say your company website was *www.webuyhousespeterborough.co.uk*. I've just typed "we buy houses Peterborough" into Google and 1,580,000 results appeared, yet *www. webuyhousespeterborough.co.uk* is nowhere near the first page of search results. Why? PAY PER CLICK. The websites that get pushed to the top of Google searches are the ones that pay the most per click in advertising – they can afford to pay more, as you are doing their leafletting for them.

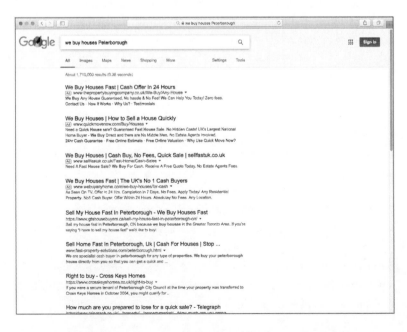

By putting your website details on your leaflet, what you have actually done is spent money on designing leaflets, on printing leaflets and on distributing leaflets only to lose your deal to the competition – you have done their marketing for them. If you just put a phone number on the leaflet, the homeowner can only contact you directly and nobody can steal your deal. I'm not saying don't have a website, what I'm saying is you need to keep your online marketing online and your offline marketing offline.

Then comes my favourite mistake: how and when you do your leaflet delivery. Many people don't have time to deliver their own leaflets and even if they do have time, delivering leaflets might not be the best use of it, so instead they hire a company to do the leaflet distribution. Now, there are two ways to get a company to drop your leaflets: individually or in bulk, where they drop your leaflet at the same time as they drop several other companies' leaflets. Let's say you choose in bulk because it's cheaper. The leaflet distribution company drops the leaflets around 11am on a Tuesday or Wednesday, while the homeowner is out at work or just out for the day. When they come home in the evening, they are welcomed by a bunch of 'junk mail' inside the front door. Have you ever come home in the evening to a bunch of junk mail? Let's be honest, it usually goes straight in the bin! So dropping leaflets in bulk is not the best way to get a high response rate.

Let's look at getting them distributed individually by a company instead: you pay the company extra to drop the leaflets individually and they do exactly as you paid them, dropping the leaflets individually at 10am on a Tuesday or Wednesday. Then an hour later, the bulk distribution company comes along and drops their bulk drop in the same letterbox. When the homeowner arrives home in the evening, are they going to be able to tell the difference, or even care about which leaflets were dropped individually and which ones were dropped in bulk? NO, your leaflet ends up in the same place as all the others, in the bin!

So how do you do leafletting correctly?

Let's start with the design. Firstly, a leaflet must be presented in a certain way to get the best response – this is called the AIDA model, which is:

A – Attention grabber

I – Interest

D – Desire

A – Action

A well laid out leaflet must follow the AIDA model to get the best response. You start with the attention grabber – e.g., "Do you want to sell your house?" Then you need to pique the vendors' interest, e.g., "I'm looking to buy houses in your area." Next you need to raise their desire to call you, e.g., "I'm willing to pay market value for the right property" and "I'm not in any chain and can move quickly", and finally, the call to action, e.g., Please call Kevin NOW on.

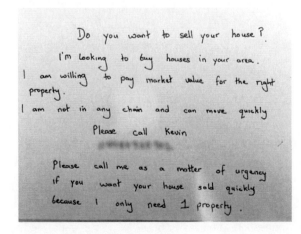

Example leaflet following the AIDA model

There is no need to write on both sides of the leaflet; I see a lot of people doing this to promote two different things, such as "we buy houses" on the front and "guaranteed rent" on the back, but I would advise to stay away from this as it can lead to confusion about what service you offer, and a confused mind doesn't buy. The other thing I see on a lot of leaflets is "commissions paid for a referral", which often includes the amount of commission on offer. This can work, but the negative to this is that it can put people off ringing you as they may perceive that you are going to give them a very low offer because you have all these commissions to pay.

Once you've got the design right, you need to get them printed. I've seen lots of information about leaflets and what type of paper to print them on, what size they should be, etc., but to be honest, paper is paper; it's not nearly as important as what is written on the leaflet and the method and time of distribution. When it comes to printing the leaflet, the only thing I focus on it the best deal, and for that reason I don't always use the same leaflet printing company, I just Google "cheap leaflet printing" and go with the company that has the best offer when I need new leaflets. Companies run different promotions at different times, so shop around.

Then we move on to the distribution. We know that deciding between a bulk drop or individual drop via a company is not that relevant, as either way the leaflet will end up on the same floor in someone's home along with a load of others, and they might never even get to see yours. Therefore, the important factor is not how the leaflet is dropped, but when. I have done numerous trials in different areas, and the best time to drop a leaflet to get the maximum response is in the evening between 7pm and 9pm or on a Sunday afternoon between 2pm and 7pm. Why? Because the homeowner gets home from work around 6-6:30pm. They come in the front door and are often stressed out from a long day at work, and have just been stuck in traffic or on public transport. They pick up all the 'junk mail', go straight to the bin and throw it away! Then they might go upstairs and get changed or have a shower or cook dinner, and they start to relax into their evening.

It's at this point that you want them to receive your leaflet. They hear the letterbox rattle and they might wonder who's that at this time of night? They walk towards the front door and notice your leaflet on the floor. You now have a small time window in which you have their sole attention – the critical time is between them walking towards the front door to pick up the piece of paper sitting on the floor and them taking that piece of paper to the bin. Don't be mistaken, their first thought is still bin it and this is why your 'attention grabber' is so important – they always glance at the leaflet on the way to the bin, and if they see something that piques their interest, they will read more!

How do you do an individual leaflet drop most efficiently in the evenings? You can either do it yourself, hire a company to individually drop your leaflets during these times or source your own leaflet dropper. I have found that doing it yourself or hiring your own leaflet distribution person works best. I can hear some of you reading this now thinking to yourselves NO WAY AM I DROPPING MY OWN LEAFLETS and you're right, you don't want to be doing it all yourself. However, it is always a good idea to do some yourself. Why? To learn how long it should take, but more importantly, it massively helps you learn your investment area, as you get to know the streets inside out. Once you have done a bit of leaflet dropping yourself, then you should quickly outsource to your own leaflet distribution person.

What's the best way to source your own leafletting person? If can be difficult to trust someone to drop your leaflets correctly and not just throw them in the bin, so what I always recommend is to park on a street and watch whoever is dropping leaflets – if you watch them drop a leaflet in 20+ properties and they don't skip a single door, then approach them and ask them if they are doing it for themselves or not. If they are dropping leaflets for another person or company, then ask them if they would be interested in some more work. Now you have yourself a leaflet distribution person who you can trust for a fraction of the cost of a company.

The final key to a successful leaflet marketing campaign is how many leaflets you drop and the frequency of the drops. The worst thing you could possibly do is blanket drop an area of 20,000+ houses, it just doesn't work. Remember the seven points of contact? People need to see your message much more often before deciding to ring you. I recommend dropping no more than 2,000 leaflets at a time, then every four weeks drop another 2,000 leaflets to the very same houses, and continue to do this month after month. Don't change the leaflet, keep it the same or at the most change one or two words; the idea is to build mind space, and to do this you need the homeowner to associate the newly-distributed leaflet with the ones they've received in previous months. When they see your message regularly, then they start to perceive you as an established company and not just some fly by night chancer.

If anyone ever tells you again that leaflets don't work, it's likely because they have never done it or not done it correctly! Leaflets are no different to anything in life, there is a system that works for everything, and if you follow the system used by successful people who have implemented it before you, then success will also come to you.

3. Direct mail

Direct Mail is one of the very best methods of targeting motivated sellers, but like any of the other strategies, there is a system to doing it correctly to maximise your conversion rates. Have you ever received a marketing letter from a company such as a broadband provider or utilities company? I'm pretty sure the answer is yes, but why do they do it? BECAUSE IT WORKS! Although most of the time we might throw those letters in the bin, not everyone does.

Apart from thinking direct mail doesn't work and therefore not sending the letters, the next biggest mistake we can make is to believe it can work and do it in the very same way as the big companies do – i.e., brand our envelopes and address them "to the homeowner". This will dramatically reduce your conversions. Why? Because there are certain times when you want to be perceived as a big company and certain times when you don't, and this is one of the times when you don't. People on the street know the names of the big broadband and utilities companies so the company doesn't even need the letters to be opened to achieve their goal of building mind space. We need the homeowner to open our letters. But not only that, a lot of properties are either tenanted or empty, and post is viewed by the tenants, letting agents or estate agents, and when they see a letter addressed "To the homeowner" with a "we buy houses" type company logo, the letter gets chucked in the bin.

I have a lot of properties that are managed via our letting agency and other agencies, and I always receive any post that is addressed to me personally. Agents are instructed to pass post onto the landlord and if it's an empty property on the market for sale, the homeowner has usually set up a post redirection service with the post office.

To maximise the likelihood of getting your letter opened, you should always make it look personal, keep all branding off the envelope and hand writing the details of the homeowner – for example, address it to Kevin McDonnell and never write Mr. or Mrs., as this is too formal. If post is collected by a letting or estate agent, you want to maximise the chance of that letter being passed to the homeowner without being opened, so it needs to look like a personal letter from a family member or a love letter.

This letter is one I received from a local property investor; although it was very good, it could have been improved by writing my first name as "Kevin" and not "K" and removing Mr.

How did I receive the letter and what made me open it? Well, inside our front door we have a letter holder where all unopened letters are placed, and I always check here when I walk through the front door. This one afternoon when I arrived home, there was a purple letter standing up in front of the letter holder, kind of taking pride of place in the entrance hallway. Before I had a chance to even pick it up, I heard my wife shout "letter for you!" from the kitchen. I replied, "yes I can see it" and almost faster than the speed of light she replied back "well are you not going to open it then?" So I opened the letter and made her wonder for a few more minutes what was written on it before I showed it to her. Why did the letter work so well? Because it looked like a love letter! You need to make your letters stand out from the normal marketing junk.

How do you determine who to send the direct mail letters to? If you are looking for properties to do Rent2Rent, then you can get the HMO register from your local council – this register will include the name and address of the landlord. You can then write the letter directly to them. If you are looking to target motivated sellers, then you can write letters directly to any address you see on the market for sale with agents, properties advertised for sale by the owner (see below) and empty properties; we ask our leaflet distributer to record the addresses of all properties that look run down or empty when they are doing their leaflet drop and we then target these addresses with our direct mail campaign.

4. For sale by owner boards

'For sale by owner' boards are signs placed by the homeowner either in their house window or in front of their property, offering their property for sale. You might be thinking *how is this marketing for motivated sellers?* But if you see one of these signs, it massively increases the likelihood that the seller is motivated and may be in financial difficulty, as they are desperately marketing to sell their home privately, possibly because they can't afford the agent's fees. This may be due to having little or no equity in the property, therefore making it a possible lease option or Rent2Rent deal. The person who does our leafletting records the addresses of any properties they see with a 'for sale by owner' sign. This is another example of why it's so important to do more than one form of marketing, as a lot of them link together.

For sale by owner sign

5. Knocking on doors

Knocking on doors gives us the best conversions of all the marketing strategies. Why? Because if there is a 'for sale' board outside and the homeowner is in, then you are talking directly to the vendor the minute they open the door. If they are motivated to sell, then they will be delighted that you're standing on their doorstep; if they are not motivated, then you can easily see this by their reaction to you being there, which will save you countless hours of wasted time chasing a deal that was never a deal. The best time to knock on a door is in the evening after the agencies are closed. When someone answers the door, ask if they are the homeowner and say you were just driving past and saw the sign and are looking to arrange a viewing. Say that you'd tried the agent's number on the board but they seemed to be closed, and ask if you could arrange a viewing, "or is now a bad time?" If they are a motivated seller, now will not be a bad time. If they advise you to ring the agent in the morning, then it's likely that there is no deal to be had.

6. Bandit boards and sandwich A-boards

Bandit boards and A-boards are a great way to gain mind space as they are different and snap people out of their day-to-day routine for a few moments – long enough for your message to sink in and generate a response. You need to be aware, though, that there are certain areas of the country where councils can fine you for bandit boarding, so I recommend you Google the "clean neighbourhoods act" and find out what your local council's policy is on this strategy. If you do put a mobile phone number of the boards, them make sure it's not your personal number – buy a SIM card at a local shop and use this number or use a short code number; you can find short code number providers on Google. With a short code number, you don't pay for the number, you pay for the code. For example, your code might be text "HOUSE" to 44444 or text "SELL" to 44444 – it's the word you are buying and not necessarily the number.

When you purchase the short code number, anyone who texts it will have their details passed onto you, so again, make sure the number used for passing the messages on is a separate SIM card and not your personal number.

Bandit board

Sandwich boards, also known as A-boards, are another brilliant way of targeting motivated sellers. A company famous for using this form of marketing is Domino's Pizza; why would a multinational company like Domino's use A-Boards for marketing? Simply because it works!

How do you make sandwich boarding work best for finding motivated property sellers? It works best when used in conjunction with leaflets, because if you or one of your employees are standing on a street wearing a sandwich board, very few, if any, people will approach you in public and tell you they are struggling and need to sell their house quickly. What they will do is take your contact details and speak to you in private later, but they will likely be too embarrassed to even ask for your contact details. You need to give your details to them, so you get someone to stand on the street in a busy part of town, like outside the train station, shopping centre or football stadium for example, wearing a sandwich board to attract attention, and you get them to hand out leaflets to everyone who passes buy. This is perfectly legal as long as you are in a public area and have a policy to pick up any leaflets that people drop on the street.

Would anyone really wear a sandwich board in public? Domino's doesn't seem to have a problem recruiting people, so you can too! Why not start by approaching one of the Domino's pizza sandwich board employees and asking them if they want any extra work?

Sandwich A-boards

7. Word of mouth / recommendations

I cannot emphasise enough how powerful word of mouth and recommendations can be when negotiating with sellers. If you are trying to negotiate with someone on anything in life and they have never met you before and don't know anyone who knows you, it can be more difficult to build trust and credibility than if someone recommended you. I have one sign in particular that comes to mind: it's located directly across the road from a pub, and the landlady of the pub can see the sign every day when she looks out the window from where she stands behind the bar. Lots of customers go to pubs to have a few drinks and drown their sorrows, and they end up talking to the landlady about their personal circumstances and problems. On numerous occasions I've had calls from motivated sellers who have said the lady in the pub told them to ring; I have even had calls from people while they were sitting at the bar in the pub! I have now helped these people with their property problems– some by securing a deal on their properties and some by giving them advice on the best thing for them to do in their current situation if their property didn't suit my criteria. The landlady now stands behind the bar, points out the window and says "ring that number, he has helped other people". I pop into the pub every few months and thank her. If a seller rings me but we can't help them, or their property isn't right for us, we always give them advice to help them and they then reciprocate by recommending us to other people they speak to who might need help.

MARKETING FOR TENANTS:

Letting agents

Leverage your local lettings agents to find you the best tenants. They already do the marketing and have the skillset, so unless you plan to manage your own properties or open your own agency, then use a good local agent. I don't recommend managing your own portfolio unless it's just to gain some knowledge around how it works; I used to manage my own properties when I started out and all it did was drain my time from higher income generating tasks. I thought I was saving money, and I was, but in reality I was saving the pennies and missing out on the pounds.

Your long-term plan may be to open your own lettings agency and create another income stream, but the best time to do this is likely to be when you get to the financial tipping point, where it becomes cheaper to open your own agency and have your own staff manage your property than it would be to give them to another agency to manage. At this point, headhunt the very best staff from the other agencies in your area. To do this, you need to identify who the best agency staff in your area are, which is another reason to use a few different agents now and not put all your properties with one agency.

Social media

Social media platforms such as Facebook are a brilliant resource for finding tenants. There are buy, sell, rent and house share groups set up by local people in pretty much every town in the country, where local people offer and look for properties to rent. If you use this resource, you will never be short of tenants for your properties.

Word of mouth and incentives

Tell everyone what you do and ask them to recommend people to you who are looking for accommodation; we get about 20% of our tenants from recommendations now. A great way to get recommendations is to offer people an incentive to recommend you to people looking for accommodation. We offer current tenants a cash incentive if someone they recommend moves into a property. This works especially well in multi-let properties, as the current tenants will find people who they want to live with, which means there will be a lower turnover of tenants, plus you'll have a much better idea of whether the person they recommend will be a good tenant who pays based on your experience of the person recommending them.

Websites

Either have your own website or leverage other people's websites, such as spareroom.co.uk to find room let tenants or Rightmove, Zoopla or OnTheMarket for single let tenants.

Recruitment companies

Aim to build a relationship with local recruitment companies in your area; their job is to find and place people in jobs, and in a lot of cases this involves getting jobs for people who are out of the area, so being able to offer accommodation as well as a job helps them secure the applicant. In return, you can direct people looking for accommodation and current tenants to the recruitment company should they need a job. This is a great WIN-WIN for both businesses.

Local factories

Most factories have communal staff areas with canteens, restrooms and changing rooms, and often in these areas there are notice boards displaying offers and local services to employees. Speak to reception and ask if you can have a postcard and notice displayed on the board, or get a current tenant or someone you know who works for the company to display your notice for you.

Local shops

Similar to the local factories, lots of local shops have notice boards where you can display your room for rent or property for rent signs. Have some signs printed and get someone to go to all the local shops and put signs up on their notice boards, then put a system in place to go around each of the shops once a month to make sure the signs are still displayed, replacing them if not.

MARKETING FOR TENANT BUYERS

Mortgage brokers

Mortgage brokers are a great source of potential tenant buyers. Their job is to speak to people who are looking to get mortgages to buy or refinance a property, and on a lot of occasions people who speak to them want to be homeowners but for various reasons cannot qualify for a mortgage yet. You can help these people with your Rent2Own programme. Can you speak to mortgage brokers and get them to give you the details of everyone on their books who failed to qualify for a mortgage? Unfortunately, NO! Under the General Data Protection Regulation (GDPR) it would be illegal for them to pass a client's details on to you without approval. So, what can you do? You can get to know one or more mortgage brokers well and explain what you do (high-level, not detail – you risk them doing it for themselves if you teach them the detail). Give the mortgage broker your permission to pass your details on to anyone who fails to qualify for a mortgage. This is great WIN-WIN-WIN as the mortgage broker gets to maintain the client and get them a mortgage in the future, you are being recommended by the mortgage broker so the initial barriers like trust are already lowered with the client, and the client gets the opportunity to become a homeowner.

Social media ads

Just like with marketing for tenants, social media platforms such as Facebook are a brilliant resource for finding tenant buyers, but the best way to use social media for tenant buyers is doing ads. For just a few pounds, you can directly target people who are actively looking to get on or up the property ladder. You can create an ad that specifically targets people by age, social demographic, location and interests. Your ad can include keywords such as mortgages, finance, home move, mortgage broker, etc., and if any person has done an online search or showed interest online for anything relating to these subjects, your targeted ad offering Rent2Own will appear on their social media platform. It's the equivalent of leafletting but on the web.

Postcards

Postcards are another great way to market for tenant buyers. Lots of local shops, takeaways and supermarkets have display boards for placing postcards, and although some charge a small fee to display a card, most are free. Get a few hundred postcards printed, similar to the one below, and send someone around all the shops in your investment area once a month to get them displayed. It can take a few hours the first time you do this, and you need to speak to the shop owner or staff to get permission the first time, but then each month it's just a matter of popping back in to make sure the card is still displayed and if not, to put a new one up. Some shops charge weekly, so just pay for four or five weeks when you put it up, so you don't need to visit every week.

Postcard

Estate agents

Lots of people visit agencies every single day looking to buy a property or just having a look to see what's available, but don't have enough funds available for a purchase. Agents take their details and put them on their database, but the reason most agents ask for proof of funds before doing a viewing is that if they didn't, they would waste a lot of time doing viewings with people who didn't have enough to buy the house. Unfortunately, just like with mortgage brokers you can't just get a list of these people from the agents due to GDPR, but you can ask the agents to pass your details on to the people who enquire about buying a house but don't have enough funds. This can be a great WIN-WIN-WIN-WIN as you can secure the purchase of the house, so the seller gets their house sold, the agent gets their commission, you get a tenant buyer and a property deal, making you a profit, and the tenant buyer gets the opportunity to become a homeowner.

Signs on cars

This might seem a bit random, but signs on cars are a great way of attracting tenant buyers. Remember – tell everyone what you do! Having a sign on your car allows you to be continuously marketing for tenant buyers everywhere you go. If your car is rarely in the area where you are looking to invest, then ask to have signs put on someone else's car or buy an old car and park it in the area, so people get to see your message every day. If you are buying an old car and parking it in the area, make sure it is taxed and insured and have someone move it around every few days, or you risk having it broken into if locals notice it parked in the same place for days.

Rent2Own board outside a property

You don't need to spend a fortune on expensive signs and advertising to attract your target market; some of my most successful marketing has been something cheap I have done that stands out and looks different to the normal day-to-day things people are used to seeing. For example, just getting a cheap piece of plywood and writing "Rent2Own" on it with a mobile phone number has generated many more calls from tenant buyers than a professional-looking estate agency board; this is because people don't notice the professional boards as much, as they don't interrupt the pattern of daily life. If you place a Rent2Own board outside a property, you will be inundated with applications. Why? Because the average age of a first-time buyer is increasing every year, and most people cannot afford to buy a home or move up the property ladder from the home they currently live in. They are not used to seeing these signs on every street like estate agency boards, and they see it as an opportunity to finally get on the property ladder.

Board

Newspaper ads

Newspaper ads work great, especially in the papers that also advertise properties for sale or rent. If you place an ad in one of those papers, then you can directly target the people who like to look through the property sections of the papers. However, never pay the rate card price – always negotiate! A newspaper has a sales team and they are often on a salary plus commission, so they need to secure a certain amount of sales per month, both in monetary terms and add space sold. If you offer to take the same section of a paper but for a long period of time, for example 3-12 months, then you can get a significant discount, as the ad space will be included in the sales person's total monthly sales for calculating their current month's commissions and bonuses, even though it's spread over a longer period.

Marketing for private finance and JV partners

Have you heard the saying "if you find the right deal the money will find you"? Well that's a load of rubbish, if you find the right deal the money won't find you! The money will only find you if people know you are looking for it. I'm going to cover the different ways of raising other people's money in chapter 13, but what I want to do now is focus on how to market for private finance and JV partners. You need to tell everyone what you do – there should not be anyone within 10 feet of you, either online or offline, who doesn't know you invest in property. If you do the following, you will have people coming to you looking to invest money without ever having to ask:

Networking events – business and property

The number one way to raise finance to grow your business is through networking. The saying "your network equals your net worth" is so true. It may surprise you to know that I'm an introvert, and when I was first told I needed to network, I was thinking *NO WAY – I'll do other things, but I'm not going to some meeting and chatting to a bunch of strangers*. Just a few years later, I'm standing on stage running my own events. In my first few years in property, I only attended a few networking events and tried to avoid talking to people. Whenever there was a break, I'd sneak off to the toilets or to the bar for a drink to try and avoid people, and if I was in the room with people near me, I would be on my phone so I wouldn't get caught up in a conversation. There was one event where I was standing in the corner of a room on my phone trying to look busy and then my phone rang and I almost dropped it in panic, it was so embarrassing! The reason I'm sharing this is because just like anything else, networking is a learnt skill. Everything is always more difficult in our heads than it ever is in reality.

My top tips for networking:

- Don't worry about the fact that you are just starting out, just be yourself and people will relate to you and be attracted to you.

- Never try and sell to someone at a networking event, you have only just met them.

- Don't spend all evening talking to one or two people and miss everyone else. Your aim is to collect as many contact details as possible to build your network; you then have the rest of your life to build relationships with those people. If they leave the room without you getting their details, you might never see them again.

- Don't ever give out your business card without getting one back in return, as they might never contact you. It's not important how many cards you give out, what's important is how many you collect.

- Follow up with each contact by calling them a few days later and find out what it is they are looking to do in property or business.

- Invite them to your area for an 'investors' day' to showcase your area, your knowledge of the area and the profit potential from deals.

- Don't just go to property events, go to other types of business events as well. At a property event, you can build contacts that can help you, but most people are also learning to build a property business. However, at business events you will meet people who are interested in investing in property but don't know how.

Property events

What I mean by property events as opposed to property networking events is that property events are things like property sale exhibition events and property training events. How are these different to networking events? Because at a property sale exhibition, the people who attend are looking to buy property, they have the funds available but are still not really sure what they want. This is your opportunity to promote you and your business. Property training events are a higher level than networking events, as they are often paid events and at least one or two days long, so you have automatically qualified the people in the room – if someone has invested the time and money to attend a one or two-day event, they are proving they're serious about property. What's more, a lot of high net worth individuals attend these events just to find someone who has got the right investment knowledge to work with them – they invest their money in return for your time. This is not just true for one or two-day events, but also higher-level events; I run a mentoring and mastermind program, and there are people who join the program just to find people to lend their money to. They want the security of knowing that the people they are lending to are the very best, and joining the mentoring and mastermind program is their way of qualifying those people.

Social media

Social media has made the world so much smaller – it allows us to be within the click of a button of virtually anything we need. If you are not yet using social media to grow your business, then you need to start TODAY! When I say social media, I mean all the different platforms, such as Facebook, Twitter, Instagram, YouTube, Pinterest and LinkedIn, and I will include a personal website in this section, as all your social media platforms should link to your website. You don't need to set them all up at once, but you do need to start with one and have a plan to get them all up and running.

In today's world, if you can't be found on social media then you don't exist. You could meet someone at an event and come across really accomplished in what you do, but they will then look for you online to find out more about you, and if they can't find anything or if what they find doesn't align to the you they spoke to at the event, then this could destroy your opportunity to raise funds. For example, your Facebook page might be full of pictures of your dinner and nothing about property; I know they are called 'social media' platforms but if you want to grow your business and raise funds, you need to use them as 'promote my business' platforms. There needs to be a balance of business and personal life online, so a potential JV partner can learn about the type of person you are in all aspects of your life. Social media is your shop window – make sure you display yourself in the best light.

Charity balls, social events and members' clubs

Charity balls, social events and members' clubs are a brilliant way to find private investors and JV partners, as people who attend these are generally quite wealthy. The main reason these are great places to find people is that you get to speak to them in a non-business environment, so they aren't as guarded or dismissive of you, which means you can get to know them without them feeling that they are being pitched to. Places like flying clubs, yacht clubs and the Institute of Directors are full of wealthy businesspeople who often have an interest in property but don't have the time or knowledge to invest. You are the missing piece of the jigsaw for them.

Business angel events

Business angel events are similar to Dragon's Den, where people go and pitch their business ideas to the angels, looking for investment. You can use these to either pitch your business plan to the angels or just attend for the networking and meet people in the room. You should always be looking to give the perception that you are not chasing the money and that you don't need it; if you push people away they will want you more. It's like taking a toy from a baby, they will cry until they get it back. My top tip if you are attending these events is to attend to watch and not pitch – just sit in the room with the high net worth individuals and strike up a conversation with them. They will more comfortable talking to you if you create the perception that you are not after their money, and this gives you an opportunity to get to know them, and them you. Remember: don't chase the money and never ask for it on the first date.

Signs on cars

This may seem a bit random and not in line with all the other approaches I have just discussed, but the reason I've included it is because it works! Tell everyone what you do, and what better way to do that than signwriting your car. Now don't panic, you can either have it professionally done or you can buy magnetic signs online that can be removed whenever you feel the need. I know we are talking about ways to raise finance or JV partners, so when I say signs on your cars, don't go out and buy a sign that says "I need your money" – I'm talking about signs that say "we buy houses". Don't be mistaken by thinking this just attracts motivated sellers, it also attracts people who are interested in property investing and they will often approach you to ask what exactly it is that you do. When they do that, exchange contact details and arrange to meet them for a coffee.

Podcasts

Podcast are a massively growing market – people want to be able to access content quickly and more and more are turning to podcasts, as they can tune in and listen to what they want to, whenever and wherever they are. You don't have to plan your life around podcasts, you can plan them around your life. They connect you with your target market. The other great thing about podcasts is you can put your message out to the world and the haters cannot comment as there is no way to leave comments, so they just go away and do their hating elsewhere. You can either run your own podcast or you can be interviewed on other people's. Either way, you'll be positioning yourself as an expert and people will connect with you and want to know more about what you do.

We have covered a variety of different marketing techniques in this chapter, some of which you will love the idea of and some of which you might have read and thought *no way am I doing that*. That's fine, you don't need to do everything, but you do need to do something. Make sure that whenever you are marketing, you do more than one form of marketing at a time – it's about mind space and getting people to see your message as often as possible. Once you get your marketing campaigns up and running, leads will start flowing in and it will be time to secure some deals, so in the next chapter we will cover negotiation

Case study: For sale by owner board

I have a local handyman whose job is to go around all my properties and carry out any small repairs, and while he's doing this, I ask him to keep an eye out for any properties that are for sale by the owner. He sent me a picture of a sign at a property one evening so I rang the number displayed on the sign and a guy answered the phone. I asked him if he would be interested in selling the property and he said he was looking to sell it for £85K because, although they hadn't instructed an agent yet, they'd had agents round for a look and they had valued it at £85K. I knew the street and knew that in good condition it might be worth about £80-85K, so I would be looking to secure it for less. I informed him that I would be would be looking to pay £70-£75K for the property and he immediately

Hi,
I rang last week to enquire about your house for sale, I was sure you said it was valued at £85k but I've just seen it marketed for £79950.. it's a shame you went with agents as I had said when I called that I was thinking £70-75K.. if you did still want to sell privately you would save on the agents fees..
Let me know if you want to discuss again
Regards
Kevin

Hiya mate. I am away this weekend, will text you early next week to discuss if thats ok.

said no way, not a chance! A few weeks later, I saw the property for sale on Rightmove for £79,950 so I sent him a text message:

"Hi, I rang last week to enquire about your house for sale, I was sure you said it was valued at £85k but I've just seen it marketed for £79,950. It's a shame you went with agents as I had said when I called that I was thinking £70-75k. If you did still want to sell privately you would save on the agents fees. Let me know if you want to discuss again, Regards, Kevin

Within a few minutes he had replied saying "Hiya Mate. I am away this weekend, will text you early next week to discuss if that's ok"

I immediately knew that I was getting a deal, I was suddenly his "mate". I know had the higher ground in the negotiation as he had lied to me about the valuation and he knew I knew, so from that point on we were able to discuss the deal with honesty. It turned out that the property wasn't even his and that he was just doing the viewings on behalf of his partner. She had a £67K mortgage on the property and just wanted it sold – she was now living with her partner and had rented the property out but didn't have consent to let, and when the tenants moved out she decided to sell and not re-let. But she was now covering two mortgages while it sat empty. Although I had initially said I would pay between £70-75K for the house, I eventually bought it for £69K. How and why? Partly because he had lied to me – I didn't want to pay as much, so when he came back to me I said that the money I had available was now tied up in another deal, so the maximum offer I could make was £69K. The lesson here is don't worry about having to reduce a price if you need to, you need to do what's right for you.

Case study: Steven Meyer

The following are Steven's words:

I attended Kevin's No Money Down and Rent2Rent training and though all the creative strategies are useful, the Rent2Own (tenant buyers) strategy stood out. Having recently bought my house the 'normal' way, I could see how this strategy would work well in my area of High Wycombe (South Bucks). Like much of the South East, property prices have soared. This strategy could help people struggling to get a deposit to get on the property ladder.

I started out targeting and building a list of tenant buyers using the creative marketing techniques Kevin had taught us. One such technique was sign writing for cars. This was good, since I would be driving locally to viewings and my J.O.B.

I followed his advice for small, stand-out leaflets and went bigger. A week or so later I had large yellow and black signage: two magnets and one sticker. The sticker announced I BUY HOUSES for finding sellers, and the magnets RENT2OWN for tenant buyers. Both have produced leads over time, but the sticker got the best result the very next day.

I had parked on the high street, and when I returned to my car, somebody knocked on the window. I opened the door expecting complaints about my parking. "I see you buy houses. I want to buy some houses." I hadn't expected that, and it caught me off-guard. I expected people with houses to sell to contact me, but this elderly gentleman had seen somebody who knows how to buy houses. They say that perception is reality; this proved it to me. Now I'm helping this man keep his money from Corbyn (his words) and he's funding houses for me.

Of course, we didn't come to this arrangement immediately. I grabbed a business card and pen from my car and wrote his phone number down. Later we met up in a Waitrose café (this is the South!) and I learnt about his investing preferences. These were capital growth and commercial properties – not what I wanted. Further meetings furnished details such as no leaseholds, and he guided me in finding out about land deals. At the end of one lunch, I introduced the concept of tenant buyers, with the enhanced yields and potential exits. By the next meeting, he'd become taken by the idea and was keen to get some tenant buyers. It took five or six meetings to get to this point – me bringing some properties to prove myself and talking through legal packs.

Kevin never seems to run out of ideas, though. I've also found, on his suggestion, lots of other sources of tenant buyers, too.

Whilst it may be helpful to start with lots of cash, Kevin has shown that there are plenty of ways to start without lots of cash. Did I mention that my investor has over £2M to invest? Get your message out there and ALWAYS carry a pen and business cards, even in the car!

Chapter 7: Negotiation

Being able to negotiate is a key skill for successful Investors, as it can mean the difference between securing the deal you want under the terms you want and potentially losing the deal or paying too much for it. Yet it is often the one area of investing that people shy away from and are uncomfortable with. Negotiation is no different than any other part of your business, in that there is a system for how to negotiate to get the best deals, you just need to know what steps to follow and then practise, practise, practise until you become an expert at it. There is not a successful person on this planet, in any walk of life, who hasn't had to fail numerous times before getting it right. "Every winner was once a beginner and every master was once a disaster" – Rob Moore. The difference between the most successful people and the rest is that the most successful understand they need to make mistakes and fail sometimes, but that if they keep going and don't quit, they will eventually become a master and achieve their goals.

There are many forms of negotiation in various different parts of your life. In reality, we are all negotiating on different things with different people – and with ourselves, in our own heads – numerous times a day, from choosing what to wear, what to eat or where to eat, to bigger things like marriage or divorce, we negotiate in our jobs, with councils, in government... the list goes on and on and on. Negotiation plays a fundamental part in our lives.

A negotiation is a dialogue between two or more people or parties with the intention of reaching an agreed beneficial outcome. In any negotiation, there will be points that each party differs on from the outset, and potentially new points of difference can be identified at any point during the negotiation. The aim of the negotiation is to reach an agreement on those points to satisfy all parties. Generally this means that concessions must be agreed by all involved on different aspects of the topic.

In this chapter, I will talk you through the process of a successful property investment negotiation and the principles you need to follow. You will make mistakes along the way, but every mistake is learning, and I guarantee if you stick it out for the course, you will become a master property negotiator.

Negotiating via estate agents and letting agents:

You can secure great property deals via an estate agent without ever speaking to a property owner; the role of the agent is to position themselves in the middle of the deal and negotiate an agreed outcome that suits both parties. In most cases, the agent is paid by the seller, so it could be perceived that they are working for the seller – in most cases the structure of the contract is a percentage of the purchase price, which implies that the agent has a vested interest in getting the highest price possible for the property to maximise their commission. However, there are a number of things to consider, such as:

- Have the agents got a higher than normal number of properties on their books and they want to have a quick turnaround

- Is the agent's contract with the vendor coming to an end and they are worried about losing the property to a competing agency?

- Is it coming towards the end of the month, financial quarter or financial year and does the agency need to get some sales through the books? Or in the reverse, do they need to hold some sales back until the next reporting period, e.g. to stop them crossing the VAT threshold?

- Is the agent's business model to get lots of properties on their books at a low price and sell quickly, or is it to tell vendors that they can achieve a high price for their property to get them on the books and then manage their expectations down over time once the agency agreement is in place?

- The member of staff you are negotiating with at the agency might be trying to get a couple of extra sales completed quickly so that they can beat the other sales negotiator in the office or another regional office to the 'top salesperson award' for the period. One sale could be the difference between winning an agency award and not winning it – the prestige and the potential financial gain on the award.

- A member of staff might be thinking of leaving the agency or already be on notice, and is looking to get some more sales competed quickly before leaving. Or in the reverse, they might be leaving for a competing agency and since they have a good relationship with some vendors, they are planning on approaching them to move their property over to the new agency once they have moved.

These are some of the various things you need to consider when looking to secure a deal via an agency. Sometimes when you're negotiating on a deal with an agent, the offer you are making or the terms you are offering might be perfect for the seller, but the timing of your offer might be wrong due to any one of the factors listed above. It's important to understand these factors, as they often play a critical role in whether you have an offer accepted or not, especially when we are looking to use creative No Money Down tools.

Your focus needs to be on building a good relationship with the members of staff at the estate and letting agencies; remember, property is a people business and contrary to what you may believe, estate agents are people. Make sure they know who you are – build mind space with them, visit regularly. I don't care how much money you have, or tell them you have, unless you are visiting them regularly you won't be in the forefront of their minds. When a deal comes in they will think of the person they spoke to most recently and inform them of the deal first. You want the agents to know you, remember you and be rooting for you to get a deal if there is more than one interested party. To achieve this, you need to focus on the relationship: what can you do to stand out? There are thousands of things you can do, but here are some to get you thinking along the right lines:

- Visit at the same time every week so they start to expect you and know you for coming at that time

- Bring sweets or chocolate

- Do some unexpected, random things like baking cakes instead of bringing chocolates for no reason

- Always bring a bottle of champagne or something after a deal has completed; a great tip is to ask another member of staff what the agent you are dealing with likes to drink and get them their favourite drink

- Ask them about holidays, weekends, etc. – most people just talk property, but you want to build a friendship

- If you see them on a night out, buy them a drink

- If you are selling any properties, offer to sell them via the agency to give them extra commission

- If you do any viewings direct to vendor (D2V) and the deal is not right for you, recommend the agency to the vendor and the agents will likely reciprocate this later

- Ask the agents what you can do for them – often they will be getting pressure from a vendor about not having enough viewings on their property, so simply agreeing to do a viewing and give feedback, even if it's a property you are not interested in, can help the agent

I know some of you are reading this thinking *what has this got to do with negotiation? It has everything to do with negotiation*, because if you can get the agents on side, they will work for you and do the negotiation for you with the vendors. Remember, the agent's job is to be the middle person – their job title is often Sales Negotiator! However, you want to get to the position where the agents trust you to do the viewings directly with the vendor, as no matter how good an agent is at negotiation, they don't know what you know and they don't understand creative strategies. Very few agents are property investors themselves and most are commission-based salespeople whose job is to sell a house. You are a professional property investor who understands that you cannot build a scalable property business quickly unless you are using creative techniques, and if you try and explain the process to an agent who then has to re-explain it to a vendor, some critical aspects of the offer will be lost in translation.

More importantly, they won't know how to handle objections from the vendor and will respond to objections with comments like, "I don't know, I'll find out". Instead of building a feeling of comfort with the vendor, they will automatically make the vendor feel uncomfortable about an offer that was likely the best solution for them. Put yourself in the vendor's position and ask the agent a question about an offer; if the vendor says, "I don't know, I'll find out", immediately you may be thinking *well, if they don't know and they are the agent then it must be risky*. This is why in negotiation you should focus on building a great relationship with the agents with the aim of them allowing you to negotiate directly with the vendor.

Negotiating direct to vendor (D2V)

You can get some great deals via estate agents and letting agents; however, the best deals are generally always achieved direct to vendor (D2V). Now when I say D2V I mean leads you have created from your D2V marketing campaigns. If you are informed of a potential deal by an agent, you should never cut them out of the deal – always pay your agents, and pay them well, as they will then be incentivised to bring you more deals. However, what you should aim to do, wherever possible, is cut them out of the negotiation. When explaining creative NMD strategies to vendors, they will always have questions and objections and you need to be there to handle these and give them the confidence that structuring the deal in a particular way is the best for them. Focus on solving the vendor's problem and you will get the deal. The biggest mistake people make in negotiation is only focusing on what they want and not on solving the vendor's problem.

If you approach every negotiation with the mindset of 'I'm here to help' and focus on a WIN-WIN result, you will massively increase your own wealth whilst helping people solve their problems. I have developed a six-step formula to winning in negotiation that anyone can follow, it's the six steps to a RESULT:

Step 1. Rapport

Rapport with the vendor is arguably the most important part of a creative property negotiation. I have emphasised many times that property is a people business, and this is never more evident than when negotiating with a vendor on a creative solution to selling their home. Rapport needs to start from the moment you first speak to them, whether that's in person or on the phone, and it needs to continue right through to the end of the process. You need to make it personal right from the outset; the initial introduction can win or lose you a deal.

Introduce yourself on first name terms and make sure you refer to them using their first name.

Me: **"Hi, I'm Kevin, great to meet you. May I ask your name?"**

Vendor: *"It's Bob."*

Me: **"How can I help, Bob? May I call you Bob?"**

Vendor: *"Yes, that's fine, thanks."*

Once the introductions are out of the way, you need to focus on listening to the other person's problem and finding out as much as possible about them and why they are selling. Look things you have in common, like similar interests in politics, sports, hobbies, etc. All the time you're doing this, you are automatically building rapport.

I remember at one property I viewed D2V, the lady offered me a cup of coffee and a biscuit and as soon as I picked the biscuit up in my hand I could tell it was stale. Now when I was younger, my Mum always used to say to me that if you are ever offered something to eat in someone else's home it's not polite if you don't eat all of it. So, I was sitting there with this stale biscuit thinking about what my Mum said and thinking *if I don't finish this biscuit they will think I'm rude and I will lose rapport and the deal*, so I finished the biscuit. Guess what happens when you finish a biscuit? You get offered a second one. I was thinking, YIKES, why do I listen to my Mum? So, thinking quickly, I said, "I'm ok thanks, when I leave I've got to get dinner", to which she replied, "would you like to stay for dinner?" Was I getting the deal? You bet I was!

Step 2. Empathise

When you do D2V negotiations you will come across various different scenarios explaining why people are selling their properties. Often there will be a reason that's difficult for them to talk about and may not seem important to you, but when you're speaking to the vendor, it's the most important thing in the world to them. If you are very 'me-focussed', only interested in securing a deal and not worried about the other person, then this will lose you the deal. A great negotiator needs to be a great listener; my Mum always says, "You have two ears and one mouth so use them in that order". There is nothing truer than this when it comes to negotiation.

An example of not empathising:

You: "Do you mind me asking why you are selling your home?"

Vendor: "I've lost my job."

You: "You've lost your job. Really? That was a bit stupid, wasn't it?"

Ok, I know I've exaggerated my response slightly for effect, but can you see that by giving a negative response and not making their job loss the most important thing in the conversation that you have missed the opportunity to empathise and build rapport? Most, if not all, other people who come to view their house will have shown no interest in the fact that they've lost their job; by showing you care about them, you differentiate yourself in a positive way from the competition.

Now let's look at the same conversation, but this time you show empathy:

You: **"Do you mind me asking why you are selling your home?"**

Vendor: *"I've lost my job."*

You: **"I'm sorry to hear that, I've lost my job a couple of times in the past and I know it can be a difficult time. Would it be ok if I could have a chat with you for a few minutes about your current situation and see if there is anything I can do to help? I can't guarantee you that I can help but I have helped other people who have lost jobs, so if I can get a good understanding of your situation maybe there is a solution that can help you, would that be ok?"**

Vendor: *"Yes, that would be great."*

Step 3. Situation

People sell properties for a variety of different reasons, and it's not your job to question why, it is your job to find out why! What I mean by it's not your job to question why is that students who attend my training regularly ask why someone would agree to a creative strategy because they wouldn't. DON'T THINK EVERYONE THINKS LIKE YOU!

Not everyone thinks like us; we are all unique in our own ways, not everyone wants to be a property investor and not everyone believes they can be successful – if they did, then nobody would sell a house, they would just rent them out and make a profit instead of selling today. Why is any house on the market? As educated property investors, we know that if we buy a property at the right price we can make a passive income from it, so why doesn't the seller just do the same thing?

It's not for us to question why! What you need to do is put yourself in the shoes of the vendor and aim to identify everything you possibly can about their current situation, both personally and financially, so you can work out how you can help them. There are literally hundreds of reasons why someone may want to sell their property, and some of the reasons may mean that no matter how much you want the property there is just no deal to be had. For example, they are mortgage-free with a large income and no real need to sell, and they're just testing the market to see if they can get the highest price possible – in this scenario, don't waste your time, just move on.

You job is to identify the situations that are likely to mean the seller is motivated to agree to creative terms on a property. As I said, there are literally hundreds of reasons why someone may be open to a creative solution to selling, and some of these include:

- Divorce

- Moving abroad

- Job move

- Couple moving in together, leaving one house empty

- Previous sale fell through

- Property run down

- Distressed landlord

Step 4. Understanding

Once you get the vendor to open up about their current situation, you need to work out which one of the NMD tools is the best one to solve their problem, while also working for you. At this point you can sometimes get drawn into helping someone simply because their situation strikes an emotional chord with you, so you must be careful that although you are trying to help them in the best possible way that you also don't agree to a deal that's not financially viable for you. Although property is a people business, and by focusing on solving other people's problems you will have massive success, it is also still a business! You can't allow yourself to help someone at the detriment to your own business, no matter how emotionally connected you become – there are just some situations where you cannot help. Focus on getting a deep understanding of the different tools, such as assisted sales, lease options, vendor finance, EDCs, Rent2Rent, Rent2Own, etc., so that you know when it's right to use each tool and when you can use more than one tool to structure the same deal. If you only have one way of securing a deal, such as a BMV offer, that's like a plumber walking into a property to fix a leaking tap with nothing more than a lump hammer – you make the problem bigger. You need to have your NMD toolbox of solutions in your head.

Step 5. Learning

I believe you either earn or you learn, but you never fail. There is no such thing as failure; we go through life with a feeling of failure every time something goes wrong and then one day we get something right in a life-changing way and people suddenly call us lucky! NO! There is no such thing as failure or luck. Luck is Labour Under the Correct Knowledge. The secret to success is aligning yourself to successful people who can help you get to the next level – learn from them, work with them and then go out and follow the things they did to be successful and avoid the things that they got wrong. It's not smart to learn from your mistakes; it's smarter than not learning from your mistakes and doing the same thing over and over again, but it's still not smart. The smartest people learn from other people's mistakes. Why make your own mistakes when you could have listened to and learnt from others and avoided those mistakes in the first place?

I lost a small fortune in my early days in property because I went out and made massive mistakes, but at least I've learnt from them, and now I understand that you need to follow the successful and success will follow. The only thing I did right in my first 10 years in property to keep going. It's important to understand that you will make mistakes, but you need to ensure they are small, like saying the wrong thing in a negotiation or forgetting to say the right thing. These things happen. What you have to do is just accept them and move on knowing that if you keep taking positive steps forward you will reach your goals. You won't get a deal every time you do a negotiation, but if you follow the steps in this chapter and build a good knowledge of the tools, then you will massively increase your deal conversion ratio and become a very successful property investor.

Step 6. Time

Time is the final step of the process to getting a successful RESULT in a negotiation. In my first 10 years in property, I focused on quantity, thinking it was important to do as many viewings as possible as quickly as possible, so I would only spend up to 15 minutes on a viewing. But this led to very few results. The problem with doing 15-minute viewings is that you cannot build rapport, empathise, find out a person's situation or get a good understanding of the situation in just a few minutes. Spending enough time on a viewing is a fundamental part of success. If you focus on the quality of the viewings instead of the quantity of viewings, your results will significantly improve. Book out a full evening to do a viewing – it's much better to book out four hours to do one viewing and secure one deal that makes you £20K+ profit than it is to do 16 viewings in the same time and get no deals.

Once you know which NMD tool – or combination of tools – is the right one for the situation, it's time to start to structure the offer. There are four steps to follow:

Step 1. Building the offer

Your aim when building the offer is to work out how much money the vendor needs to move on. Don't just look at the mortgage debt, there are other things you need to consider too, such as other liabilities they may have, like credit cards, personal loans, car finance, etc. Try and help structure a deal in which all these debts are taken care of. The worst thing you could do is to agree a creative deal like a lease option with a vendor only to find out a few weeks later, after you have spent time and money on the deal, that they had a second charge loan secured against the property you didn't know about.

You don't need to agree a deal on your first visit. When starting out, this can be daunting, so I have broken the process down into plan for you to follow over three meetings with the vendor. As you practise, improve and grow in confidence, you can build up to securing the deals in two meetings and then one meeting.

- First visit

    1. Connect with them, build rapport

    2. Try to buy if you can but don't push it

    3. Listen – fact find – understand the situation

    4. Empathise

    5. Gently explain the options available to them

- Second visit

    1. Answer their questions

    2. Letter of authority if you need to speak to their lender

- Third visit

  1. Sign Head of Terms

  2. Send to solicitor

Step 2. Making the offer

You should make an offer on every property you view. What would be the point in going to do the viewing if you didn't make an offer? I see a lot of people who are busy viewing properties but don't offer on any or most of them. Why not? If you don't offer, you don't know if you could have got a great deal. There are generally only two reasons why people don't offer. One is that they only know how to look at a deal in the traditional way and base the value on how much they can purchase it for today, rather than investing in themselves by learning the tools you are reading about in this book. The second reason is that often they are afraid of having their offer rejected. There is nothing wrong with having your offer rejected; the first "no" is not the end of the negotiation, it's often the starting point of the objection handling process. We know the vendor wants to sell or rent the house, right? Because they either had it on the market or replied to your marketing. So if they reject your offer, then it's not that they don't want to sell, it's because they have an objection that you need to overcome.

Step 3. Test close and handling objections

When negotiating, you don't want to just blurt out an offer and leave it open to a "yes" or "no". The secret to a successful negotiation is testing the close to get a feeling for how likely it is that the vendor will say yes. The best way to do this is through objection handling. There will always be some objections, and your ability to fish these out and answer them will determine if you can get to a yes.

Don't get excited, chuck a load of different options for buying the property at the homeowner and expect them to choose – not only will they not know which one to pick, but they will get confused and overwhelmed, and a confused mind cannot make a decision. You need to determine which NMD tool can help them in their current situation and is right for you, and then make them two offers:

The first offer is always a BMV purchase for 75% or less of the asking price, and the second offer is a creative strategy using one of the NMD tools. How you position this is as follows:

Offer 1:   Your terms   –   My price

Offer 2:   Your price   –   My terms

The reason for this is that 99% of people only know of one way to do a property deal, i.e. sell for a price they are happy with today, so their starting point (their terms) is always, "I want my money now".

You make them two offers:

- Offer 1 is "you can have your terms, which is your money today, but it's my price, which will be 75% or less of the asking price".

- Offer 2 is "you can have your asking price, but if you want your asking then it's my terms, which is we will give you some money now (such as your equity) and give you the rest later, possibly in a few years' time (which is clearing their debt – the mortgage)".

By making two offers, it's no longer a yes or no response, it's now a choice between offer 1 and offer 2. You position this by saying "based on what you have told me, I believe the best solution for you in your current situation is [offer 1 or offer 2] – which do you prefer?"

Before making the two offers, you need to make sure you have handled any potential objections – you don't want the objections to be raised during the offer stage. The following two questions are used for fishing out potential objections:

- Is there anything else that could stop us getting to an agreement today?

- If I was to offer X, could we get to an agreement today?

The better you have done the groundwork of building rapport and showing them that you understand what you're talking about, the more they will trust that you can deliver on your proposed solution, massively increasing your potential for securing the deal.

Step 4. Closing the deal

When you close a deal at the end of the negotiation, neither party is legally bound to it. You are not legally bound until contracts are signed – whether that be exchange of contracts on a purchase, signing of contracts on an R2R, R2O, LO or any other type of deal. This is why the six steps to a RESULT are so important, as these are the things that help ensure the vendor does not change their mind in the period between saying yes and the signing of the contracts. I always agree deals on a handshake or a handshake and signing of a Heads of Terms (HoT) document, which lists the key points you have agreed, such as:

- Address of the property

- Purchase price

- When the purchase will complete, e.g. if an option it may be years

- Who will pay for what in the interim

However, the HoT is not a legally binding document and not really worth the paper it's written on; the only reason for it is to give the vendor a feeling of security that the deal is done, and to increase the likelihood that the deal will not fall apart between you leaving the meeting and signing the actual contract paperwork once it's prepared by the solicitor. As well as signing the HoT, it's vital that you touch base with the vendor to update them on progress every few days to ensure they know you are still there and everything is ok, and to ensure the vendor doesn't get cold feet or change their mind for any reason once an agreement is reached.

Chapter 8: Exchange with Delayed Completion

An Exchange with Delayed Completion (EDC) is very similar to a lease option (LO) – they are structured about 90% the same way – but there are some very specific things that make them fundamentally different. With a lease option, you have the option but not the obligation to buy the vendor's home; if you choose to purchase the property at any point during the contract period, they are obligated to sell. With an EDC, you exchange contracts at the start, which means that you are now obligated to purchase the property and the vendor is obligated to sell. Exchange of contracts could then potentially trigger the requirement to pay stamp duty, so you need to factor this into your calculations.

Substantial completion

If you refer to the gov.uk website (https://www.gov.uk/stamp-duty-land-tax), it clearly states that stamp duty is payable within 30 days of completion. However, the website is written based on the traditional way of buying property and does not account for creative strategies. Solicitors don't work to what is written on the gov.uk website, they work to The Law Society requirements, which state that stamp duty is payable within 30 days of "substantial completion". This is where it becomes debatable: what is substantial completion? Is it exchange or is it completion or is it neither? Most solicitors will consider substantial completion to be when keys are transferred to the new owner after the exchange of contracts. If keys are passed to you on a lease option deal, this is not "substantial completion" as contracts have not been exchanged, so you're not legally bound to buy. Once contracts have been exchanged and keys have been received, this would be deemed substantial completion and trigger the payment of stamp duty, where appropriate. Remember stamp duty is only payable once and will have to be paid at some point anyway, so if you pay it upfront and the rate of stamp duty taxes increase in the future, you won't have to pay the higher rate.

I have seen numerous people debate when stamp duty is payable, saying it's payable on completion and referring people to the gov.uk website to back up their argument. Generally this is because with 99% of transactions it is true – we are used to solicitors requesting stamp duty funds at the same time as they request deposit funds when doing a traditional purchase. However, EDCs are different and there is a fine line between determining what is "substantial completion" and what is not – I always advise that you use a solicitor who is experienced in doing EDC contracts and follow their advice on when to pay the stamp duty, and to confirm what your stamp duty liability is.

You can also check what stamp duty payments are due on a property here: *www.stampdutycalculator.org.uk*.

Cases when you don't need to pay stamp duty on an exchange of contracts

Back-to-back deals. Why? Because you exchange contracts but don't receive the keys. Back-to-back deals are transactions where you agree a price with the vendor for their property, and agree a separate, higher price with a buyer. You then need to buy and sell the property simultaneously – like a buy to flip – except the transaction is done in one minute rather over several months. The key to a back-to-back deal is to have another solicitor in the middle, who can:

- Exchange on the property you are buying from the vendor at the same time as you exchange the same property with the investor.

- Complete the transaction with the vendor, after which they will complete the transaction, at the higher price, with the buyer.

Some words of wisdom on back-to-back deals: you need to find the right, commercially-minded solicitor who will understand the transaction. They usually have other solicitors they work with regularly, and you want to have two like-minded solicitors acting together, one for you and one for the vendor.

The end buyer must almost always be a cash buyer. This is because the buyer's solicitor has an obligation to disclose back-to-back transactions to a mortgage lender, most of which will not allow the transaction. This is because the vendor, in this case you, hasn't OWNED the property for six months – a standard rule among lenders, known as the 'six-month rule', which has been in place since the 2008 crash. Remember in the mid-2000s when same-day refinances were permitted? It's the same rule that prevents back-to-back deals with lenders.

The lenders also don't like the fact that they are effectively valuing the property at higher than the purchase price. Lenders will lend on the lower of the purchase price or the value of a property. If they were to know that the property sold for, say, £10,000 less only a few moments before their buyer bought it, then they wouldn't approve a mortgage for the buyer. Therefore, only look to do back-to-back deals with a cash buyer who is happy to hold the property for six months and then refinance onto a mortgage product.

One other thing to be aware of with back-to-back deals is the increased solicitor costs. You will want to pay for the vendor's solicitor in this case, to be sure they have the right solicitor and to have good control over the transaction. You will then need to pay for the solicitor in the middle, to complete on both the purchase and the sale of the property. A solicitor who is unfamiliar with this process will try and charge you the full set of fees for both, which could be upwards of £2,000! However, with a bit of negotiation and building the right relationships, you can get this down to a much more reasonable figure, as all the solicitor in the middle really has to do is forward the enquiries from the buyer, through them, to the seller, and send back their replies.

EDC with the purchase being subject to approval of application for planning gain. Why? Because you didn't receive the keys. With an EDC where you are purchasing land or property subject to planning permission, there is no need to receive the keys until after the planning permission has been approved (unless you want to use part of the agreed property purchased in the interim). If the planning permission is rejected, you have the option to give the property back, should you wish to do so – this is known as a 'conditional exchange'. If you choose to continue with the purchase, then this may then be deemed substantial completion, triggering the requirement to pay stamp duty.

What else do you need to be aware of with an EDC?

One of the key differences between an LO and an EDC is that you are legally responsible for the buildings insurance from the point of exchange with an EDC. Although I always recommend you should pay for the buildings insurance on an LO deal, you are not actually legally required to do so. However, once you exchange contracts, you become legally responsible so should any damage occur to the property, such as fire or water damage, etc., the costs of repairs are legally your responsibility.

Another key point is that more solicitors and estate agents understand EDCs than LOs. With lease options, you need to recommend that the vendor uses a specialist lease options solicitor, and sometimes this can put the vendor, and often the agents, off of agreeing to a deal, as they want to use their own solicitor. It can also put negative thoughts in their mind about the legality of what you are proposing; although it is a perfectly legal strategy when done correctly, it is still something that's new to them. Estate agents are very familiar with EDCs and how they work, although in most cases these are short term EDCs and are often referred to as a 'keys undertaking', where the purchaser can be issued with the keys and access to the property during the period between exchange and completion to begin or complete refurbishment works on the property. Agents see this as safe to do, as you have exchanged and are now legally responsible for the property, so any damage you cause would be your responsibility and covered by your building's insurance. Although agents mainly understand short-term EDCs of a few weeks, we are often looking to do more long-term EDCs from a few months to several years, so it's much easier to explain the concept to an agent or vendor than it is to explain a lease option – the only real difference between an EDC and a normal purchase is the timeframe.

Vendors often prefer an EDC over an option as it means you are fully committed to the purchase. When I'm negotiating a lease option deal, the final objection that I get from a vendor is often "what if you pull out of the deal later?" The best way to handle this objection is to offer to exchange contracts so you are now obligated to buy – this is a comfort blanket for the vendor that swings the deal in your favour.

Even though you are exchanging contracts and stamp duty may or may not be payable, depending on whether your solicitor sees it as substantial completion or not, you can still make the contract assignable, so you can pass on your EDCs agreement to another person in the same way that an option agreement can be passed on.

How do I decide if I just go with a lease option or if I do an EDC?

I believe you should never enter into a lease option contract with a vendor unless you are 100% committed to purchasing the property, as you are playing with people's lives – you are pretty much promising them you will buy their house, even if you haven't actually promised that you will complete the purchase. 99% of the time, they see the property as sold, then a few months or years later, they end up getting the house back and can't understand why. A good rule of thumb is that if you feel you would not be willing to exchange contracts on a property and be obligated to buy it, then you should also not agree to an option to buy it. The lease option gives you the benefit of being able to get control of a property for little or no money, but it should not be a tool that you use to take advantage of people and make money from a property that you fully intend to give back.

If you are putting a large deposit down on a property (your money, investor funds or tenant buyer funds), I would always recommend exchanging contracts to protect the money. With a lease option, even though the vendor is obligated to sell, there is always still a risk that they could challenge the contract in court and potentially win. This is not a big risk, but it's important that you are aware that the risk still exists. If you have put little or no money into an LO deal, then the worst-case scenario would be that you would lose the property but not lose any money. By exchanging contracts, you guarantee the vendor is obligated to sell.

If you are placing a tenant buyer into a property, then I would recommend you exchange contracts, as this protects the tenant buyer's interest in the property. Imagine a scenario in which you have promised a tenant buyer that they can rent the property with the option of one day owning it and they go ahead. They not only get emotionally invested in the deal but also financially invested – they may have cosmetically of structurally improved the property. What if they were then one day told, "sorry the vendor has challenged the option to buy agreement in court and we have lost so you need to leave now"?

If there is a large refurb required or if you are adding value and you will be investing a lot of money in the property, then I would always recommend exchanging contracts to fully protect your investment. You can exchange contracts and then undertake a refurbishment to improve the property and add value, then choose to either purchase the property or sell the property at its new improved value by assigning your contract to another person.

The above are worst-case scenarios, and the likelihood of them occurring are extremely slim. However, I would be doing you a disservice if I didn't share all the risks with you as well as the rewards. I see so many so-called gurus teach people various property strategies and make it all seem so easy, yet they never share the potential downsides. I just don't agree with that. Like anything in life, there are upsides and downsides, and it's important to be aware of the potential downsides so you can put systems, processes and contracts in place to mitigate the risks. Ensuring you use a specialist solicitor will protect you; they are the experts and they get paid to think about the things that you either don't know or miss, and they can ensure you are protected as much as possible.

What do I need to consider before entering into an EDC agreement?

Unlike a lease option, you cannot walk away from an EDC deal without risking significant costs (unless it's a conditional exchange, as discussed earlier), so there are a number of things you need to consider before entering into an EDC agreement to ensure you are in a position to complete the purchase at some point in the future. The key things to consider are as follows:

- How are you going to fund the purchase in the future? At some point, you will need to buy the property, so you need to be very clear on how you are going to fund the purchase. Will it be your own money, other people's money or via a tenant buyer, for example? (I will be covering how to raise other people's Money in chapter 13).

- At what point in the future are you aiming to complete the purchase? Is it in a few months' time or a few years' time? Be very clear on this so you can them start to plan around the funding of the deal.

- If your plan is to purchase the property with a mortgage, what happens if lenders change their lending criteria or if you have a negative mark on your credit file in the future that restricts your ability to borrow money? Always have a back-up plan in place.

- How long is remaining on the vendors mortgage? If the vendor only has six years left on their mortgage and you are planning on completing the purchase more than six years in the future, then this just won't work, as the mortgage lender will be calling in the loan at the end of the agreed mortgage terms; if you are not in a position to buy, then the lender can force a repossession in order to sell the property to release their funds.

The importance of speaking direct to vendor and why it's often easier to do deals with professional investors:

I often hear people say they can't get creative deals through to completion via agents and others who believe it's difficult to get a good deal from another investor.

The below might help with both those beliefs...

I viewed a property via agents and wanted to secure it on a lease option; I explained the process to the agent without mentioning the words lease option: "I will agree the purchase price now, and then I will babysit the vendor's mortgage for a period of time and complete the transaction later. The vendor will get their equity now and you (the agent) will get your commission". Based on this, the agent was happy to put the offer forward. The vendor accepted the offer and then a few days later the agent rang me back saying the vendor was unhappy and just wanted a straight sale, and that his solicitors were not happy either. I asked the agent if it would be ok for me to meet the vendor in person to explain my reasons for the offer and so he could see I was genuine. The agent agreed and allowed me to meet the vendor alone (importance of building a good relationship with your agents).

I met the vendor at the property on a Saturday morning; my plan was to talk him through an option where I was happy to exchange contracts but delay completion. We met at 11am, he showed me around and we ended up back in the living room. I was about to explain to him my reasons for wanting a lease option when he said, "I see two ways forward here, the first is a lease option and the second is an EDC, have you heard of them?"

It turns out the vendor was an experienced investor with a large commercial portfolio and wanting rid of his only single let – he had done options before and even used the same solicitor as I used, small world! 10 minutes later, both of us are happy, handshakes done and a 12-month EDC agreed with a WIN-WIN for both of us – he gets his equity upfront and I get time to get in and refurb, release funds that are currently tied up in another deal, buy cash later once funds are released and then refinance onto a mortgage product at the increased value price, releasing my funds again for the next deal.

Lessons:

1. Had I not gone direct to vendor, the deal would most likely have fallen through, as agents don't know what we know and therefore don't know how to present it, even if we get them to put the offer forward.

2. It's often easier to work with experienced investors, as they understand creative deals.

3. You don't need money today to buy property, you need the right knowledge to be creative and focus on the 'terms' that work for both you and the vendor, but focus on solving the vendors problem/need first.

Case study: Exchange with delayed completion

I was contacted via Facebook by the niece of a lady who owned a 2-bed semi-detached house in my area. She had heard from a friend of hers that I bought houses and asked if I might be interested in her Auntie's house, so I arranged a viewing for the next evening. The property was a 2-bed ex-local authority house with a large garden that needed a cosmetic refurbishment. The owner was in her mid-60s, working part-time, and could afford the property payments but wanted to sell and move into rental. Although she could afford the monthly running costs, she couldn't afford to pay for a refurbishment and was worried that if anything expensive happened, like the boiler breaking down, she wouldn't be able to afford to replace it.

However, although the costs of repairs were a worry, her main motivation for selling was that her son was in and out of prison, and when he was out he kept coming back to the property, causing damage and bringing trouble to the house. The poor lady wanted to move to a place where her own son couldn't find her. She had identified a lovely property to rent in a nearby village that suited her needs, and she didn't want to miss out on it.

I agreed a deal where I would pay her deposit and first month's rent to secure the property immediately, which came to just under £1,000. I did this on trust, as I just felt the deal would be ok, and if anything went wrong I would get the deposit money back anyway, so I was only really risking one month's rent of £350.

The property was worth approximately £70,000 and she had an outstanding mortgage balance of £56,261. She was paying £300.11 a month on a repayment mortgage (capital and interest). We agreed a purchase price of £59,261; I would give her £3,000 today to move on, then take over her £56,261 mortgage and babysit her monthly mortgage payments. We would exchange contracts but delay the completion, allowing me to complete the purchase at any point in the next 12 years and the purchase price would be what was remaining on the mortgage at the point of exercising the option to buy. As it was a repayment mortgage, each month I made the £300.11 mortgage payment, the overall mortgage balance of £56,261 was going down by just over £200 per month.

The numbers:

- Market value: £70,000

- Purchase Price in 12 years: the remaining mortgage balance

- Mortgage: £56,261

- Monthly mortgage: £300.11

- Market rent: £450

I then placed a tenant buyer in the property with an option to buy at £85,000 any time in the next five years. The tenant buyer agreed to pay £450 market rent plus £150 per month option consideration top-up and a £3,000 upfront option consideration. Both the upfront and monthly option consideration money are credited towards the purchase should they exercise their option to buy, and non-refundable should they not. The £3,000 covered the money I agreed to give to the vendor to release her from the property, making it a No Money Down deal for me.

The numbers:

- Option consideration top-up: £150

- Option fee: £3,000

- Purchase price in five years: £85,000

Case study: Maria Thomson and Claire Yew

Claire and Maria standing in front of the Building – Warriston Place

This is a ground floor retail with a basement as its storage area, purchased on an exchange with delayed completion deal subject to planning permission. JV funding from Claire was used for the purchase once planning permission was approved, making it a No Money Down deal for Maria. The following are Claire's words:

Maria had found this property, which had been on the market for some time, with an asking price of £225,000. The vendor had retired and ceased business in the property. After some negotiation by Maria, the vendor agreed to submit and pay for a full planning application to change it from commercial to residential. The planning application was for three units of 2-bedroom flats.

At this point, due to the uncertainty of planning, about £100,000 of equity was needed to complete the purchase with bridging finance. Maria got in touch with me and I agreed to be her JV partner and fund the £100,000 for a 50% share.

In order to secure the deal, as we were afraid that the vendor might change his mind upon planning approval, we negotiated an exchange of contracts, with the condition that we would only complete subject to obtaining planning permission for the flat conversion. That meant in the event that planning could not be obtained, we would not be obligated to complete the purchase.

Fortunately, planning permission was granted in two months, therefore we didn't require any bridging finance and were able to go straight to development finance. The soft uplift given by planning raised the value of the property from £225,000 to £260,000. Development finance took the soft uplift in value, and because of that we were able to go directly to development finance to purchase at 75% LTV. With this uplift, instead of about £100,000 only £56,000 was now required, as the planning grant took the uncertainty out of the deal, and the soft uplift of £35,000 was taken by development finance as Maria's equity share. I then agreed to fund the £56,000 for a 25% share, making this a No Money Down deal for Maria.

Once we had completed on the purchase, we applied for variation on planning to convert one of the 2-bed flats, which was substantially larger, to a 3-bed flat.

- Purchase price: £225,000

- GDV: £720,000

- First 2-bed flat: £245,000

- Second 2-bed flat: £225,000

- Third 2-bed flat: £250,000

- The third 2-bed flat would be converted to a 3-bed flat, and this would lead to a slight uplift in value.

- Total loan facility for acquisition costs, build costs, professional fees and finance costs: £507,000

- Cash invested by JV partner, Claire: £56,000

- Cash invested by Maria: £0

- Projected profits: £720,000-£507,000-£56,000 = £157,000

- 75% profit for Maria: £117,750 with No Money Down

- 25% profit for Claire = £39,250 = 78.5% ROI

Summary

In summary, EDCs are a great way to secure a deal and give the vendor piece of mind. Always think about what you want from the deal: is it short term or long term? Do you want to be tied in or do you want the flexibility of being able to easily walk away? Are you in a position to be able to pay the stamp duty upfront if required? And remember, it's not just about you, what is it that the vendor wants?

Chapter 9: Assisted Sales

An assisted sale is a powerful strategy that allows you to make Buy2Flip returns from a property without needing to own it. To grow a successful, sustainable property portfolio as quickly as possible, you need to have different strategies for cash flow, capital growth and lump sums of cash today. Buy2Flip has traditionally been the strategy used by investors to create lump sums of cash quickly, by purchasing a run-down property, or a property with scope for improvement, and then undertaking a refurbishment and/or extension before selling the property for a profit. However, there are several costs involved in this that eat up a significant amount of your potential profit, such as:

- Legal costs to purchase

- Stamp duty

- Finance costs whilst undertaking the refurbishment (even if you are buying cash, there is the missed opportunity cost of having your money tied up in a deal)

- Legal costs to sell

- Estate agents' costs to sell

- Capital gains and/or corporation tax

With an assisted sales agreement, you target the very same type of property that you would be looking for to do a Buy2Flip, but instead of buying the property you agree an assisted sale with the homeowner, in which you help them sell their property in return for a share of the profit. How this works is you agree a purchase price with the vendor and they wait an agreed period for their money; in the interim, you refurbish the property to add value. The property is then sold, they get the agreed amount and you get the difference less the costs of the work.

The great thing about an assisted sale is that in most cases, you are able to offer the vendor much more for their property than anyone else, making it not only a very profitable strategy but also ethical, as you are not trying to hammer the vendor down on price to make up your profit margin. You can often offer them more than their asking price due to the cost savings you can make by avoiding things like stamp duty and finance costs.

Why doesn't the homeowner just refurbish it themselves? Quite often it's because they can't afford to or they don't have the money, but sometimes it's simply that they can't be bothered or don't know how to go about getting the work done.

There are different ways to structure an assisted sales agreement and I will go through the key ways in this chapter. Like any strategy, there are risks and rewards, so I will explain what you need to ensure is in place to protect yourself.

Different ways to structure a deal:

You agree to help the vendor sell their property, whereby:

- You carry out some improvements at the seller's cost to help make the property more desirable to a buyer and then sell their property for an agreed share of any uplift in sale price over and above their current asking price, less the costs of the works. For example, the vendor has their property on the market for £90K but you calculate that with a £12K refurb you can make the property worth £125-130K. You agree that the vendor will invest £12K in a refurb and then on sale they get their asking price of £90K plus their £12K refurb money (£90K+£12K = £102K), then the vendor gets a percentage of anything over this price, less the selling costs.

- You agree a sale price with the vendor and then you carry out a refurbishment to add value, and any profit over and above the agreed sale price plus refurbishment costs is yours. For example, the vendor has their property on the market for £90K but you calculate that with a £12K refurb you can make the property worth £125-130K. You agree to give the vendor their asking price of £90K and you pay the £12K refurb, then on sale you get any profit over £102K. (£90K to vendor +£12K refurb = £102K).

- You agree an initial sale price with the vendor plus a percentage of the profit after refurbishment. For example, the vendor has their property on the market for £90K but you calculate that with a £12K refurb you can make the property worth £125-130K. You agree to give the vendor £90K PLUS, for example, 50% of the profit after the £90K + £12K refurb costs have been paid. You pay the £12K refurb and then on sale the vendor gets the first £90K and you get your refurb money back (£90K to vendor + £12K back to you = £102K), then you and the vendor split any profit over £102K 50% each.

- You agree an initial sale price with the vendor where they also get a percentage of the profit after you have got the costs of the refurbishment plus your minimum profit. For example, the vendor has their property on the market for £90K but you calculate that with a £12K refurb you can make the property worth £125-130K. You agree to give the vendor £90K and you pay the £12K refurb, then take the first £15K profit (£90K+£12K+£15K = £117K), then the vendor gets a percentage of anything over this price, less the selling costs.

Each of the above structures is slightly different and the key to deciding which one to go with is to ask the vendor what is best for them. They are unlikely to go for any of these unless the property is sticking on the market or unless you can show them how they can make more money by waiting a few more weeks or months to sell the house. The great thing about this strategy is that the type of property you are targeting is the very same property that you would be looking for if you were doing a Buy2Flip. This means that if you have a good understanding of assisted sales, you automatically get an unfair advantage over other investors in the area who are looking for Buy2Flip deals, as they are likely to offer vendors significantly less than their asking price. Structuring the deal as an assisted sale gives you the ability to offer the asking price for the property while the traditional Buy2Flip investor needs to include costs such as stamp duty and finance costs in their budget, meaning they can't compete with your offer.

With assisted sales there is no stamp duty, as you are not purchasing the property, and there are often no finance costs if you agree that the vendor continues to make their mortgage payments, if they have any, until completion (remember they are currently making their mortgage payments today anyway and the property is not selling, so by offering them their asking price with a few weeks or months, this will incentivise them to continue paying for a little longer as they can now see a definitive sale date).

What are the benefits for the vendor?

- They get to sell the property and move on with their lives

- They often get their asking price plus some extra

- They have a guaranteed sale agreed

- Their stress and pressure is relieved – selling a house is known to be one of the most stressful periods in a person's life

What are the benefits for you?

- You save on stamp duty costs – these savings alone can often pay for the full refurbishment

- You often don't need to organise or pay any finance costs (although this depends on how the deal is structured, as in some cases you might agree to take over all the costs, such as utilities and mortgage payments, while the property is under your control, but it's still a massive saving on applying for and taking out your own mortgage on the property)

- No capital gains tax if doing the deal in your personal name, as you are not selling the house, the vendor is

- Often no estate agency costs, as the vendor is paying these

- You don't need to tie up large lumps of capital for purchasing with cash or pay a 25% deposit

- You don't need a mortgage

- You can even structure the deal No Money Down

What are the risks and how can you mitigate them?

There are four main risks when doing an assisted sale deal:

- The vendor changes their mind and says they don't want to sell after you have spent time and money on the deal

- You fail to find a buyer for the deal in the timeframe agreed

- You find a buyer, but the best offer is lower than you had anticipated

- Unforeseen circumstances such as death, critical illness, divorce, job loss, etc.

Let's look at each one of these individually.

- **The vendor changes their mind and says they don't want to sell after you have spent time and money on the deal**. There is always a risk that the vendor decides not to sell the property, so it's important you have a tight contract in place to protect you – you should always use a solicitor who is experienced with assisted sales to draw up the contract for you. It shocks me when I see people on social media asking if they can borrow an assisted sales agreement from someone else; they do this to save a few hundred pounds in legal costs and don't think about the risks to the money being invested in the deal, which are often significantly more. Do your numbers prior to agreeing to a deal and always include solicitor costs – this is your protection. Budget for £700- £1000 in legal fees. If you would like details of a good solicitor who can help you structure these deals, send me a message on social media.

A contract is only as tight as it can be and is never belt and braces; if someone decides they want to challenge it, they can challenge it and you could end up in court, which can rack up a large bill, so don't just rely on the contract. Property is a people business and although I always use a contract, I put the majority of my focus into building rapport with the homeowner to ensure I get a good feel for the type of person they are, their situation and motivation for selling. After a couple of hours or a couple of meetings speaking to a vendor, you generally get a gut feeling about how they will act throughout the process. If you have any negative thoughts, I would advise not going ahead with the deal, as your gut feeling is generally right.

In addition to this, you can also request that any money invested in the deal is secured as a second charge against the property. However, this is subject to the current mortgage lender agreeing. Most lenders are generally ok with this but there are some lenders that won't allow it. Don't automatically assume you can just get a second charge, as it's not always the case, and lending criteria are always changing, so at the time you are reading it might be more difficult to get second charges than it is at the time I'm writing. If you do secure a second charge, then this immediately implies there has been a loan and therefore a loan agreement. Speak to a specialist solicitor about this, as loans may mean interest payments must be made on the money, etc.

The best and most widely used way to secure the deal and protect yourself is via the use of an option agreement, similar to the option agreements discussed in chapter 4. They are worded differently and have different clauses in them, as these are short-term option agreements as opposed to the longer-term agreements you would have on a lease purchase option. The assisted sales option agreement gives you the option to purchase the property during the term or assign the option to purchase to someone else – i.e. the buyer you find for the property.

- **You fail to find a buyer for the deal in the timeframe agreed**. An assisted sales agreement typically has a set timeframe specified in the agreement, so one of the biggest risks is that you underestimate the length of time it takes to sell the property, meaning you fail to find a buyer, or the buyer pulls out. The best way to mitigate this risk if you are investing money in the deal is to not spend any money on the property until you have a buyer secured and you take a non-refundable deposit from the buyer to verify their commitment and tie them in. You then use the buyer's non-refundable deposit to carry out the work, or if this money is tied up in a solicitor's account, you use the equivalent amount of money from elsewhere (personal savings, loan, JV partner funds, etc.) to carry out the work.

On a typical Buy2Flip project, you purchase the property, then carry out the refurbishment works, then market it for sale, and then once a buyer is found you start the legal process. With an assisted sale agreement in which you find the buyer first, the timeline would look like this:

1. You agree the purchase of the property in X number of weeks

2. You immediately start marketing for a buyer

3. Once the buyer is found, commence legals and they pay a holding deposit

4. At the same time as legals are taking place, you start the refurbishment works

How can this work? Why would someone agree to buy a house that's not refurbished? The reason this works is for the very same reason off-plan selling works for developers: most people don't want to buy a property and then refurbish it, they want to move into an already finished home where nothing needs doing. I've learnt this from my wife. The first house we moved to required a cosmetic refurbishment, and after the last two properties we have moved to personally, I was given strict instructions that we were not moving to another building site, LOL.

The thing about moving into an already-finished home is that it is often done up to the developer or investor's taste and not to the buyer's taste so some things always need changing. This is why off-plan purchasing works so well for developers, as people can agree the purchase off-plan, pay a holding fee to secure it legally and then be able to request specific changes from the plans to make the property look and feel how they want it.

Now take this very same off-plan model and use it for a property you have secured on an assisted sale. You don't sell the property in its current condition, you sell the dream of the buyer being able to transform the property to their taste but have all the works done for them, i.e. they can pick the kitchen they want, the bathroom suite they want, the type of flooring, the colour of the walls, the tiles, etc. Obviously, prices can vary drastically, so they must pick from an available range that you offer them to ensure it stays within budget. You then organise the completion of the refurbishment and they get the keys to their dream home once completed.

- **You find a buyer, but the best offer is lower than you had anticipated**. This is why it's important to know your numbers and be very clear on the likely sales price. Always have a best-case price, average-case price and worst-case price and make sure there is a profit in the deal for you at the worst-case scenario price point. I also recommend you follow the guidelines in step 2 above so no money is tied up in the deal until you have a sale price agreed.

- **Unforeseen circumstances such as death, critical illness, divorce, job loss etc**. One of the main things that is often overlooked when people are doing creative deals is what happens if the seller's circumstances change – or worse, they die during the period of the agreement. To ensure you protect yourself and your buyer from this risk, you must always use a competent solicitor who will secure your interest and the buyer's interest with a legally binding contract. The solicitors don't just provide a contract though; often the thing people miss when they ask for copies of contracts from other investors and just amend them to save on solicitors' fees is that the solicitors do much more for you than just provide a contract! They protect your interest in the property if unforeseen circumstances occur by ensuring things like a power of attorney (POA) and restrictions are in place.

How do you find a buyer?

The best way to find a buyer for the property is to leverage estate agents – you can use the very same agent that the vendor was using or a different agent. Estate agents are experts at selling properties, this is what they do for a living. If they weren't any good at it, they would be closed down. Your job is to be an expert at identifying deals and leveraging other people's skills to make the majority of the money. Estate agents often already have an ideal buyer on their books who is looking for a ready-to-move-into property in the area but overlooked this property due to the work required. Quite often, people overlook properties simply due to cosmetic things, such as not liking the carpets or the colour of the bathroom tiles, etc. A lot of people can't see past this – they are making an emotional decision, not an investment decision. If you are reading this book it's because you have an investor mindset, so don't make the mistake of thinking that everyone thinks like you. They don't!

Remember the agents just want to sell the property and get their commission, and although an assisted sale is a great strategy, it's not something that they will see every day, and some will never have heard of it. You need to incentivise the agents to work with you. While some agents will be happy to work with you, if they are worried about not getting a sale before the end of their agreed contract with the seller and are worried about losing the property to a competing agency, I would recommend that the best way to incentivise them is with money.

My top tip for this is to pay the agents twice – i.e. you explain to the agents that if you were to buy the house today your plan would be to refurbish it and flip in on for a profit, which would mean remarketing the property with either them or another agency, and that if they were to work with you on the assisted sale, you would guarantee them their fee on the current sale price plus an additional fee on the new sale price. They would then see double fees, and money talks. If you didn't want to offer them double fees or calculated that there wasn't enough profit in the deal to be able to do this, then the alternative would be to ask them what they are currently get paid (it will either be a fixed fee or a percentage of the sale price) then offer them a larger fixed fee or a percentage of the new sales price. For example, if the property was on the market for £200,000 and their fee was 2%, they would get £4,000 commission, but if they worked with you on an assisted sale where you added value so the new sale price was £250,000, they would get 2% of £250,000, which is £5,000. Always focus on what's in it for the other person – solve their problem and you will start to do a lot more deals and make a lot more money.

Case study: Sarah Nuttall – assisted sale using JV partner funding

The following are Sarah's words:

Having already had some success working direct to vendor and purchased BMV houses, I met a successful local investor who already had a substantial portfolio. He was intrigued by the techniques I was using to find deals and buy property and offered to pay for and distribute my leaflets to a new area that I was not yet covering in return for a 50/50 split of the deal if I did the legwork of negotiating and managing it. He would also fund the deal if required. The first lead came through on my call answering service. After I'd had my initial call with the vendor, I felt confident I would be able to come up with a solution. The owner had amassed a large amount of debt and was struggling to keep afloat, the bailiffs were coming to the house on a daily basis and he needed to sell the house, and fast.

I visited the vendor's house and spent several hours going through his finances (and masses of paperwork) – it became clear that he had enough equity in the property to pay off all of his debts and walk away with around £27K, and the deal would still stack for us too. With an assisted sale, or any direct to vendor case, it is essential that you spend this time really understanding where the vendor is financially – it is often the case that they either don't know how much debt they have, or they are choosing to kid themselves that things are not as bad as they really are. The last thing you want to do is to set up a deal which would mean they had sold their house but not managed to pay off all the debts they thought they could.

From our conversations, I knew that the owner had serious credit issues and he was also going to struggle to rent a property without having a year's rent in advance. Additionally, he was a hoarder and had no money to pay for a removals van or any real family support to help with the move. It became apparent that he was really going to struggle to move unless he was given a bit more time. I explained that there was a way in which I would be able to help him to move – he would have two weeks in which to empty the house, but he could leave behind anything he did not want to take (this was a real benefit to him). I would pay his year's rent in advance, plus deposit (around £10K) plus some other immediate bills, including his council tax arrears and car insurance (around another £5K). I also agreed that I would make his mortgage payments until the sale completed. The price we agreed was more than I would be able to offer if I were to buy the property to flip on, so we created a real win-win.

Because we were not buying the house, we were able to start the search for a rental property for the vendor to move into immediately. Fortunately, the local investor had a contact with a suitable property who was also happy to take a tenant with a cat and poor credit in return for the year's rent in advance (this is when your network can really pay off!).

We instructed the solicitors to draw up the contracts (a combination of a charge for the lent monies, declaration of trust and a power of attorney for dealing with the sale). Having a separate solicitor representing the vendor is essential.

Importantly, we did not go about refurbishing the property, as there was very strong demand for refurbishment projects in the local market. It also meant that we could be out of the deal more quickly. The only money we spent was to have the property cleared, plus the mortgage interest and legal costs.

- AGREED PRICE: £130,000

- FINAL SALE PRICE: £175,000

- COSTS (MORTAGE PAYMENTS, LEGAL COSTS, CLEARANCE, ESTATE AGENTS SALE FEE): £7,000

- TOTAL PROFIT: £38,000 (MY SHARE: £19,000)

I'm now in the process of taking control of my third assisted sale property; this strategy is a fantastic way of getting into property and creating large chunks of cash. The total profit across the three deals is projected to be £95,000. All created with either No Money Down, or very little money down. ☺

Chapter 10: Title Splitting to Add Value

Title splitting (TS) is a brilliant strategy for adding value to a property. It involves taking a unit and chopping it up into more than one unit using legal work to split up the Land Registry Titles, creating separate legal units that you can then either sell on for a profit or keep for long-term rental income. However, the great news for you is that you don't even have to own the property to title split it for a profit. Title splits can be used in conjunction with any one of these other No Money Down strategies:

- Vendor finance to title split, add value and keep or sell

- Assisted sale to title split to add value and sell

- EDC then title split to add value and keep or sell

- Purchase with JV partner funding, then title split to add value and keep or sell

- Purchase with borrowed funds, then title split to add value and keep or sell

There are lots of larger properties across the country that have been broken up into flats and then let out individually to create a higher rental yield. You must be very careful if looking to buy these and not presume that they have already been title split with the correct planning permission and building control signoff for the conversions. There are lots of these types of deals that have been done illegally without the right consents; an easy way to identify this is when they are marketed as "cash buyer only", or when you are informed by agents upon requesting a viewing that it is cash buyers only. Why cash buyers only? Because if the owner has not had permission for the conversion, then the building will not be mortgageable.

This is where there is an opportunity for you to make money by securing the deal using one of the five No Money Down strategies listed above, then get the correct approvals, title split and increase the value. If you can prove these properties have been split for longer than 10 years, you can get a certificate of lawfulness, split the titles and get leases written for each, and then either sell (if secured on an Option) or exercise your option to purchase and refinance onto a long-term mortgage product.

Splitting a property into two or more separate units:

With title splits, you are effectively splitting a property's title by retaining the freehold in one entity and creating leases for the split sections within a separate entity. It is critical that you get legal advice from a solicitor who is experienced in title splitting from the outset, as there are some very strict criteria that you must adhere to. For example, if you own a building and title split it, you cannot issue a lease to yourself; the way to get around this is to set up a limited company, purchase the property within the limited company and then issue the leases to yourself and/or your JV partner/s. You can then refinance the properties independently at a later date.

It's important to note, though, that if you are planning to title split a property and then refinance it onto a mortgage product or sell to someone who will need a mortgage, then the current minimum sized property that a lender will currently lend on is 30 square metres. (This could have changed since the time of writing, so speak to a mortgage broker to confirm the current rules.)

The best kinds of properties for title splits are generally square or rectangular with big square footage (2000-2500 sq. ft) and high ceilings. If not already split, aim to get properties you can split into four or five separate units. If you can identify properties that are rundown and not mortgageable, this will increase your ability to secure a deal using one of the NMD strategies and generate sufficient profit.

These types of properties can be found using all the methods discussed in chapter 6: Marketing, but in addition, you can find some deals with great potential at auctions and via commercial agents.

The three-step process to a No Money Down title split:

- **Agree an option to purchase**

  If you identify a property that has the potential to be title split, you can agree a price upfront and sign an option agreement to secure the right to buy the property at the agreed price before an agreed future date.

- **Apply for planning and change of use**

  Once you have agreed the option to buy, you can then apply for planning permission and change of use to split the building into individual units. You will also likely need building control approval; this is a different department to planning, so always make sure you speak to both planning and building control and put a separate application in to both, as they have different requirements and do not inform each other about applications.

- **Apply for a lawful development certificate**

  Once the works have been completed you can apply to your local planning authority for a lawful development certificate. If the works had been done without approval by the current or previous owners, you can also apply for a lawful development certificate. There are two types of lawful development certificate:

- An existing use of land or a building or an activity being carried out within a building in breach of planning conditions is lawful for planning purposes under section 191 of the Town and Country Planning Act 1990. You can find out more details here: *http://www.legislation.gov. uk/ukpga/1990/8/section/191*

- A Proposed use of land or a building, or some operations proposed to be carried out in, on over or under land, would be lawful for planning purposes under section192 of the Town and Country Planning Act 1990. You can find out more details here: *http://www.legislation.gov.uk/ukpga/1990/8/section/192*

There are some commercial lenders that would give you a mortgage on a property while it is still on one title and would then not object to you subsequently splitting the title into two or more units and even selling off some of the units whilst retaining part of the building. You would not need to redeem the original mortgage when you sold one of the title split parts (although in most cases the lender would expect most, if not all, of the sale proceeds to go towards paying down their outstanding loan, but this can be a great way of reducing your debt on a building and increasing your monthly cash flow). The main concern for the commercial lender would be that your loan to value (LTV) stayed within their allowable limits so they would likely require a revaluation of the part of the building that you had retained to satisfy them that their loan was still within the maximum LTV limit they would lend. You could only sell if they granted you consent to sell, as they would have the first charge holder on the building and their priority would be to ensure the lent funds were secure.

Title splitting is a brilliant strategy through which you identify houses with large gardens or corner plots and you agree an option to purchase the house subject to planning permission on a section of garden, and then once planning permission has been approved you can either:

- Buy the house, split the titles and do the development using other people's money

- Split the titles, sell the house and do the development using other people's money

- Split the titles, sell the development plot and buy the house using the funds from the sale of the development plot

Case study: Dan Buchan

Dan is one of the mentors on the No Money Down mastermind program I run, and together with his business partner Jamie York, he runs a property trading business doing all types of deals, from BMV to R2R, LO, AS, EDCs and everything in between. Here's a title split deal, with plenty of profit for both Dan and another investor.

We had a vendor call up one day, (called Anne, name changed for protection of the client) who needed to sell her property in order to facilitate her relocating to Scotland. I remember it well, the property was on Keighley Road in Halifax, one of the main roads out of the town, and an area undergoing some regeneration.

She had owned the property for several years. The lead came to us online, and she initially described what she was looking for – around £80,000 for the house. When we asked what the rental income was, she said it was tenanted at £1,000pcm. Now, you may realise instantly that's a 15% yield. It took a bit more digging to establish she was actually talking about THREE properties – three flats in one building.

Like many vendors, Anne was selling for emotional reasons, not financial ones. Her whole family had moved to Scotland, and she had become tired of managing three sets of tenants. She'd let her niece live in one of the flats, and the other two were rented to long-term council tenants, with the council paying the rent directly.

A title split requires more due diligence than a normal property, because:

1. You have to check the history of the property with the council – whether it has been split to building regulations is the main thing.

2. Appraising the property is harder, because there are unlikely to be direct comparables.

For number 1, the trick is to check the addresses and council tax first. This is easily checkable, public information. If the council considers the flats as separate already, there is a very good chance the property has been split effectively and is de facto three separate properties. We also downloaded the title, which we wouldn't normally do, to establish the relationship of the flats to the title. Sometimes, the addresses will appear as separate on the title, which they did in this case. Perfect! A nice easy one for the solicitors.

Number 2, appraising the property, was certainly a challenge in this case. There were no other flats for a quarter of a mile, you'd have to go half a mile away, which was too far for comparative purposes. So what did we do instead? We found the size of the flats by downloading their respective EPCs (I maintain that the ONLY thing EPCs are good for is establishing the size of a property!) and did a comparative square metre value based on local houses, adding in a bit of contingency.

The end value? £35,000 for the smallest flat, £40,000 for the next and £70,000 for the 2-bed. £145,000 in total! I couldn't believe it myself.

We sent the property to a small number of cash investors. When we have a deal like this, we know we can turn it around very quickly, and as demand would be high and conventional finance hard to get, we would only need to look at cash buyers.

I sent our builder around to view with three prospective buyers. One of the buyers turned up in a Range Rover with a gold chain to meet the vendor, which took some explaining, as we normally tell the vendor it's a professional inspection! We ended up selecting a local cash buyer we trusted well.

Some issues with the roof came to light, which would cost about £8,000 to fix, so we had to negotiate the price with the vendor and agreed £75,000. When the deal is good, there is no need to negotiate 'too hard', but there's also no reason to not bring a genuine issue to light.

We had an option agreement with the vendor at £75,000 and sold the deal to the investor for £95,000. £20,000 profit from a property we didn't own. The investor went on to spend £15,000 to modernise the properties, split the titles using a solicitor, and refinanced the units at £150,000.

And Anne was able to ride off into the sunset, less than two weeks after she'd initially enquired. As Kevin says, that's a win-win-win.

A few tips on title splits: Be confident in the end values. Issues like flying freeholds, or awkward title arrangements, can throw a spanner in the works. It's best to download the title, give it a once-over yourself, and ping it to your favourite solicitor for a quick overview, which is what we did in this case. You also need to be persistent in knowing the situation with building regulations and be thorough in establishing how much it may be to put right. Vendors with multiple properties will have split them in any number of ways, ranging from full transparency with the council to, well, no transparency with the council. 'Trust but verify', is a great mantra to live by here – if the vendor says that it's done to building regulations, trust them, but ensure it's verified with the appropriate certificates. Check that the council is aware of it and will allow the split. It's not necessarily an issue if it's not done to regulations, it just means you need to factor in the cost and permissions of putting it right.

Chapter 11: Planning Gain to Add Value

Planning gain is a strategy used to increase the value of land or property by applying for planning permission to build a new development or extend a current one – a development could be one or more properties. This increase in value mainly benefits the owner of the land or property, but you can use a few different NMD tools to secure the rights to the value increase in your name. The following NMD tools work well in conjunction with planning gain:

- Lease option and then apply for planning gain

- Purchase option subject to planning permission

- Assisted sale and then apply for planning gain

- Vendor finance and apply for planning gain

- EDC and then apply for planning gain

- Purchase with JV funding and then apply for planning gain

Depending on the size and location of the land or property, it may be subject to a levy or tax to divert some of the planning gain to the public sector; such arrangements are currently negotiated between the developer and the council, so always ensure you speak to the council planning department to find out if the land or property you are looking at may be subject to a levy or tax. These are currently covered under section 106 of the Town and Country Planning Act 1990. In Scotland, the equivalent is a Section 75 planning obligation covered under section 75 of the Town and Country Planning (Scotland) Act 1997.

There are some situations in which properties can be extended under permitted development, so you do not have to submit a formal application for planning permission. But again, always check with your local council planning department to see if the property you are looking at and the size of the planned development qualifies for permitted development.

The benefit of using planning gain in conjunction with one of the NMD tools is that it significantly reduces your initial outlay of funds, so you only have to purchase the property after the planning has been approved. You have immediately added value prior to purchase because the purchase price is agreed upfront. You don't even have to purchase the land or property, you could secure the purchase price on an option, then apply for planning gain to add value and once approved, immediately sell the property on for someone else to do the actual development. This way you benefit from the uplift in value created by the approved planning and take your profit without having to do any of the development works.

Case study: Purchase and application for planning gain using OPM

There was a building known as the Old Brewery House that had been converted into six flats by a previous owner. The property was then sold onto a property company that purchased it remotely, hired a local letting agency to manage it for them and rented it out for several years. The property was rundown and in need of a major refurbishment, so rather than doing the works themselves, the company placed it in an auction. When I viewed the property, it was in bad shape and I could only get access to two of the flats as the others were tenanted, but based on the two I viewed, it needed a complete refurbishment. I estimated that approx. £80-100K would need to be spent to get the building modernised, and based on that I worked out that the maximum price I could pay at auction would be £140K.

A few days before the auction, a property investor I know from a networking event that I host rang me up and asked if I was aware of the flats. He said he had spoken to another local investor who had viewed the flats and was interested in them but had estimated they would be worth up to £165K in their current condition. I decided to attend the auction anyway, I lined up a JV partner who agreed to put in the funds for the deposit and refurb and we got a decision in principal from a lender to lend 75% of the purchase price (buying with a mortgage via auction is not something I would recommend but I'll share more on that later). I arrived just before the lot was due to be auctioned off and stayed at the back of the room to see if I could spot the other investor in the room, but there was no sign of him.

The bidding started, and a few different people bid on the property up to about £115K and then it was just me and another lady. As the bidding crept up toward £130K and then past £130K, I started to get nervous that I would lose the deal; you have to be very careful that you don't let your emotions take over in an auction house, as you can easily find yourself paying way over the odds for a property (I found myself feeling this anger towards a total stranger who I felt was costing me money, lol). Thankfully, she stopped bidding and I secured the deal at £135K. The next day I found out that the other local Investor that I knew had approached the owner a week before the auction and offered £165K for the building, but the owner had said "no way", as they felt the building would sell for more than that. He didn't bother showing up to the auction, the lesson here is always show up!

With the building secured and a 10% deposit paid, we arranged for the mortgage lender to carry out the valuation and eight days after the auction, with only 28 days to complete under auction conditions, the valuer decided to value the building at ZERO because it was not liveable in its current condition. This is why I would never advise buying at auction unless you have the funds available. There were a couple of hours of major panic, but this is where it's important to have a mentor and a network of contacts implementing the same strategies as you to call upon when things go wrong. One of my contacts agreed to lend the 75% deposit at 1% per month until we got the building refurbished and refinanced. So now the deal involved me and my JV partner, with a 50-50 share each, and a private investor lending funds for an interest return.

On completion of the purchase, we got the keys and it was the first time I got to see inside the whole building. In addition to the six flats, there was a service door on the ground floor, and when we opened it, it held the fire alarm system. There were also two more service doors on the first floor – we opened the first one and it was a broom cupboard, then we opened the second one and it was a staircase to the roof space. There was no mention of this in the auction pack, so it looked like the previous owners were either not aware of the space in the roof or did not realise they could add value through planning gain. While we were undertaking the refurbishment works to the existing flats, we hired an architect, submitted a planning application and got approval for an additional 1-bed and 2-bed apartment in the roof space. We decided to finish the refurbishment, refinance to release our funds then hold the apartments to rent until all the JV partner's funds were released, then sell the building fully tenanted and with approved planning permission for the additional apartments so that we could maximise the return.

The numbers:

- Purchase price: £135,000

- Refurbishment and fees: £90,000

- Total costs: £225,000

- Revalue – six apartments: £285,000

- Rental as single lets (pcm): £411 x 6 = £2,470

- Mortgage on £215,887.50 (pcm): £1,135.30

- Cash flow (pcm): £1,334.70 (£667.35 each)

PLUS: Planning approved for two additional apartments (2-bed and 1-bed) in roof space

There was £9,112.50 of the JV partner's funds left in (i.e. all the money was back out apart from £9,112.50) after refinancing, so all rental income went to him until he got all his money back out, and then we placed the property back in an auction and sold for £295,000.

Profit: £70,000 to be split 50-50 so a £35,000 profit from a deal that I put zero money into, not a bad return for my time.

If you planned to do just one of these type deals every year that would be much more than the average UK salary from a single deal.

Chapter 12: Vendor Finance

Vendor finance, also known as seller finance or owner finance, is a form of lending whereby the seller (vendor) helps finance the purchase of a property by the buyer.

In a traditional property purchase, you agree a purchase price to buy a vendor's property and then buy either with cash or a mortgage. You apply to a bank or finance company for a mortgage and once the transaction is completed, your relationship with the vendor ends and you start a new relationship with the bank to which you then make the mortgage payments monthly over a number of years. In the simplest terms, vendor finance is where the vendor becomes your bank and 'lends' you the money to purchase the property. You need to be very careful how this is structured legally, as there are some grey areas, so I always recommend that you seek specialist legal advice when entering into a vendor finance deal. You should also familiarise yourself with the FCA regulations to ensure you are not doing anything that would breach the regulations: *https://www.handbook.fca.org.uk/handbook/glossary/G1887.html*

With vendor finance, you agree to pay the vendor a small deposit to secure the deal (this could be anything from £1 to tens of thousands of pounds, depending on the value of the property being purchased). You then make the remaining repayments direct to the vendor instead of to a mortgage company; the repayments may or may not include interest depending on what you agreed with the vendor.

You can get control of a property without the need for a mortgage, and the vendor retains control of the property via a first charge similar to a bank mortgage, so they can use the repossession process to get their property back should you not adhere to the terms of the agreement. Because there is no need for a mortgage, it means that if you can agree terms with the vendor, no outside third party can scupper the deal. Often conventional deals fall apart after the buyer and seller agree a purchase price but then the bank won't lend the required funds.

Vendor financing can work exceptionally well on a deal where the vendor has little or no mortgage and is looking to sell their property, and the property needs a refurbishment or has the potential to add value. You can JV with the vendor, agreeing to project manage the conversion works to value and selling the property; they finance the costs of the refurbishment by releasing equity from the property. You can borrow more than is required for the refurbishment so that you have extra money available to cover the costs of the interest on the borrowed funds during the period of the refurbishment, and then you agree a profit split once the works are completed on the property. You and the vendor become business partners until the works are complete and the property is sold. A No Money Down deal for you and another example of a WIN-WIN, as the vendor gets their property sold at a price that makes them more money than they were expecting, and you create a profit out of the uplift in value from a property you didn't have to buy or put any money into for the refurbishment works.

A lot of vendors have no plans for their money once they sell their property, and just leaving it sitting in the bank is not always the most financially wise decision, especially if inflation is higher than interest rates, as it means the money is devaluing. By leaving their money in the property and being paid interest on it, they can not only have their money secure in the bricks and mortar of the property, but they also get to make more money over time than they would have by selling the house today.

You may agree an initial period of time during which the vendor finances the deal, and then have an agreed point in the future when you apply for traditional mortgage financing and pay the vendor off with a lump sum to remove them from the relationship.

As with any strategy, there are some risks, such as a relationship breakdown between you and the vendor, although this will generally only happen if one party reneges on the terms of the agreement.

You should never enter into a vendor finance deal without getting a solicitor who is experienced in these types of transactions to draw up the vendor finance agreement for you.

Case study: Derek Pape – vendor finance

The following are Derek's words:

I've done lots of training, including No Money Down, which has totally changed my life. Up here in Hartlepool, I've adapted that training so that when I go into a vendor's house I'm looking for below market value opportunities, any of the creative strategies and even a deal in which they keep the house and we rent it out for them.

This is the story of my best deal up to now. A friend of mine is a DJ and he was doing a staff party for Tesco, so I paid his fee. which meant Tesco owed us a favour. I called in the favour and put my huge A-frame trailer at their Tesco 24-hour Extra store on the busiest roundabout in town for two weeks. On the back of that, I received a call from a very well-spoken gentleman who said "I've got a 3-bed detached bungalow on the market at £250K, would you like to come and see if you can sell it for me?"

To put this into context, I've packaged and sold around 150 properties in Hartlepool, all in the £40K to £70K price range, and these are 2- and 2-bed terraces and semis, so this was a huge step up for me. I went to see him and we chatted about the bungalow. What I found out was he'd already bought his next property for cash, he didn't have a mortgage on the bungalow and he didn't need the money straight away from the sale, as it was going in a trust for his grandkids. I explained that because the bungalow would rent out for around £900 a month the yield would be too low for my investors. So, we agreed to do a vendor finance deal, where he would become my bank, on a purchase price of £202,500. We also agreed a timescale of seven years with a three-year extension, just to give me plenty of time to get my own mortgage or sell it. I would pay 3% interest per year. That would make the total price £245,500 and I would pay £860.95 per month.

The advantage pf this for me was I didn't have to find a deposit or get a mortgage. I do have to pay the stamp duty and as soon as we complete, the bungalow is fully in my name, with the previous owner having a first charge to protect his money. The seller can move straight out and get on with his life, knowing he will get his money over time, and he also gets more than he would have done, had it stayed on the market waiting for a normal buyer (who knows what price he would have got).

The bungalow is 127 square metres internally and has two very large lounges, so one of them has become my office where two of my daughters and I run our letting agency from. I also used to rent one of the bedrooms out to a friend who does pensions and investments for £130 a month.

So how does this all end, I hear you ask? Answer 1: in somewhere between seven and 10 years, I take out my own mortgage using the equity I've built up as deposit. Answer 2: if we assume I wait 10 years and sell it (bearing in mind I'm improving the bungalow all the time and I've raised the ceiling price on the four bungalows here), let's say it's worth £350K in 10 years, I will have paid £103,314 off of the £245,500 original price so I would have lived here for 10 years and made around £200K, not bad in my eyes.

I have done some more of these, some of which I've kept myself and rented them out, some I've packaged up and sold for a fee. I hope that has helped show some of you what you can do with direct to vendor leads that aren't any good for below market value deals.

Chapter 13: Other People's Money

Up to this point, we have discussed how to get control of other people's properties with little or No Money Down. However, there are also situations in which you find a great property deal, but it requires money invested to make the deal work. The good news is it doesn't have to be your money. There is lots of money in the world, in fact there is enough money in the world to make every single person on the planet a millionaire, so if you are not currently a millionaire the reality is that someone else has your cash! Let's start to get that cash flowing towards you.

There are three things that you need to be massively successful in any business and property is no different, there are:

- Time
- Money
- Knowledge

The problem is most people, especially when starting out, only have one or maybe two of these – you might have lots of time but no money, or you might have lots of money but no time or knowledge about property.

Time:

The thing about time is that each one of us only has a finite amount, and every day that passes us by is reducing the amount we have left. The older we get and the richer we get, the more we start to appreciate and value time. Wealthy people value their time and are often looking to invest money with people who are willing to invest their time to find properties, so they can continue to increase their wealth but without having to give up their most valuable resource to do so – Time.

The wealthy realise that they cannot make more time, but you can leverage other people's time to make more money.

Money:

If you are anything like me, you will have grown up in an environment where you were taught that you need to work hard for money – money doesn't grow on trees, etc. NO! This is just not true, you don't have you work hard for money, you need to work smart for money and have money work hard for you. Plus, funnily enough, money does grow on trees – notes are made of paper, and paper is made of wood from a tree! Well, it was until we started making money from plastic as well, and guess what that means? THERE IS EVEN MORE MONEY!

Beliefs about money are arguably the biggest factor in why some people become financially successful and others don't. I had such negative money beliefs until I was in my mid-30s. I used to tell myself things like "you mind the pennies and the pounds mind themselves". The problem with this is if you are minding the pennies you miss the pounds; focus on finding the pounds and you will make more of them. One of my most limiting beliefs was "why would someone else lend me their money?" And I know some of you reading this now are thinking the same thing. The question you should be asking is why not?!

I spent my first 10 years in property trying to do everything on my own, but you just can't, it's not sustainable. Even if you have money to start with, you will run out, so having access to other people's money is fundamental to achieving accelerated growth! Maybe you are happy to just do one or two deals a year or get to 5-10 properties and not want to grow further, and that's fine – everyone has different goals, aspirations and needs. But if you want to build a large property portfolio of 100+ properties, then you will need to use other people's money to get there. It's actually not even that difficult to raise funds, because the people with the money need your time and knowledge to help them grow their money. The problem is most people pedestalise the money and see it as the most important thing, but it's not; it might be the most important thing to you, but it's never the most important thing to the person lending the money. Once I started to ask for the money, it amazed me how easy it was to raise funds. I ask people at some of the property investment trainings I run for a show of hands to see how many people have raised other people's money, and people put their hands up. Then I ask those who didn't put their hands up why they hadn't, and 95% of the time it's because they had never actually tried. I have also asked people what they think is easier: finding the deal or finding the money. It's generally a 50-50 split – some people naturally find raising money easier and some people find it easier to source deals. Both are a learnt skill, so you can achieve both if you believe in yourself and practise, but you could also joint venture with someone else who finds it easier to find the money and you can focus on finding the deals.

Knowledge:

Anyone can learn anything they set their mind to! We were all born into this world without knowing anything and have ended up where we are in life due to the environment we grew up in and the choices we have made. Each one of us has skills, whether in sport or in a job, etc. We have learnt skills that others have not learnt, but they were still all learnt. There was a time when we didn't know how to do the things we are now good at. What we did was practise and learn from others who had done those things before – we learnt to walk, we learnt to cycle, to read, to write and so on. With each and every thing we learnt in life, we had a mentor to guide us, someone who taught us those skills or someone we watched from a distance. There is nothing we don't know that we didn't learn from others who went before us. So why is it that when it comes to the most expensive investment we ever make in our lives (buying property), we try and do it without getting the right knowledge? Focus on getting the right knowledge and you will become investable.

We all sell our knowledge every day; most people are in a job where they exchange their knowledge and time for money and stay poor, as the JOB keeps them Just Over Broke!

If you want to be wealthy and no longer need to work again, then you can do it by exchanging your knowledge for other people's money.

I can hear you saying, "well there are other ways Kevin, you could win the lottery" and yes, you could, but many lottery winners go bust again within five years of winning because they never learnt how to manage and invest their money.

We are all stuck in a system; the problem for most people is that they are stuck in someone else's system, the government's system, where we are taught to get a good education, a good job and pension and then eventually retire broke. From the time we're teenagers, we are taught about credit and getting bank loans and credit cards to access goods and services that we can't afford, and this is all set up to keep us trapped in the rat race, working to exchange time for money to survive, and the only places we are taught to get money from are financial institutions. I was not taught at school to invest, to leverage, to outsource – the skills needed to become financially free. I was taught the skills to keep me in the system.

In today's world, money is so much more easily accessible than it was years ago; once you get this, you will have readily available access to more money than you can possibly invest. Let's look at the different places that you can access money.

Private investor finance:

Private investor finance is where a person lends you money for an interest return or some other form or repayment, but they don't take a share of the risk or reward from the deal.

There are two main types of private investor finance:

1. Hard money lenders

Individuals or companies who lend you money for some form of security in return. There are strict criteria to adhere to in terms of the use of the money and repayment of the money. Examples of hard money lenders would be banks for mortgages and secured loans, bridging loan companies, finance institutions, venture capitalists and professional angel investors.

2. Soft money lenders

Individuals or businesses who will lend you money with less strict qualifying criteria, and in some cases with no security required, such as unsecured loans, credit cards, family, friends, work colleagues, business opportunists and solo entrepreneurs.

Joint venture finance:

A joint venture is a business agreement in which two or more parties agree to create a new entity, with each party contributing any or all of the following:

- Assets
- Equity/money
- Skills/experience/knowledge
- Power team
- Time

You can build your property portfolio for FREE using joint venture finance, in arrangements where you bring the skills, experience, knowledge, time and power team to find the deals and your JV partner invests the funds. This allows you to do an unlimited number of property deals, as there is no limit to the number of JV partners you can work with – you set your own limit.

In my early days of investing, I never wanted to work with JV partners as I didn't want to have to answer to anyone else or give away any of the profit. But here's the thing, I didn't build a big business and I stayed stuck in my day job! Why? Because I tried to do everything myself. There is an African proverb that I now follow: "If you want to go fast, go alone. If you want to go far, go together". If you have some funds to start, you can quickly get your first few property deals, but when you go fast and alone, you trip up and fall; this is exactly what happened to me in my venture into Eastern European property investing. If you want to go far, you need to go together – you need people around you to mentor and advise you and you need people around you with funds to invest.

The benefit of doing everything yourself is that you don't have to share any of your profits with anyone else. However, the downside is you won't actually have as much profit as you would have done if you'd joint ventured. Why? If you're lucky maybe you can buy five houses on your own that give you £300 pcm income each, totalling £1,500 pcm. But if you use JV funding, you could buy 50 houses with a 50% share of each one – you would make £150 pcm from each house, giving you £150 x 50 properties = £7,500 pcm

There is an infinite upside to working with JV partners, and it saves you both time and money – two of the three critical ingredients to success. It not only allows you to expand quickly, but it also makes you recession proof! How? If you have a lot of debt and a limited supply of liquid cash when a recession hits, you could find yourself in financial difficulty; equity in property is great for the long term but it's not easy to access if you need funds quickly and can drop significantly if there is a house price crash. This is why investing for capital growth is dangerous and another form of gambling, just like the lottery. Your chances of winning are slim. But when you become your own lottery and invest other people's money for cash flow, you not only protect yourself from the dangers of a recession but it also allows you to grow rapidly during the recession, when assets can be purchased at a fraction of their value from people and companies who need to sell their assets to access cash quickly. More millionaires and billionaires are created during a recession than at any other time – they're in a growing market because they are able to access money quickly to buy bargains from others who over-leveraged.

The other major benefit of joint venturing is that it increases your network of contacts; wealthy people know other wealthy people. If you are spending your time working and socialising with wealthy people, it automatically has a positive impact on your life – you become the sum of the five people you spend the most time with.

> *"Be fearful when others are greedy and*
> *greedy when others are fearful"*
> *– Warren Buffet*

How do you joint venture?

You cannot just market to joint venture with anyone, it is a regulated industry. The regulations are mainly focussed on how you market to people and there are strict criteria for what makes an unsophisticated investor and what makes a sophisticated investor; you are only allowed to market joint ventures to sophisticated investors. I'm not going to bore you with a load of legal jargon, but you can find out everything you need to know by visiting the website www.fca.org.uk – search for FCA regulations PS 13/3 and read all about what a sophisticated investor is.

The FCA Regulations state that "Sophisticated investors are currently classified as clients with extensive investment experience and knowledge of complex instruments, who are better able to understand and evaluate the risks and potential rewards of unusual, complex and/or illiquid investments OR have an annual income of more than £100,000 OR have investable net assets of more than £250,000 not including their own home".

NOTE: These criteria are subject to review and may be updated in future so always refer to the FCA website for the latest requirements.

The FCA regulations are there to protect people and can often be seen as a block (or excuse) to getting out there and raising funds. There are some huge advantages to these regulations, such as:

- You can qualify people and cut out timewasters

- You use it as a 'legal requirement' to get proof of funds from potential investors

- You can use your knowledge of the regulations to demonstrate to potential JV partners that you know what you are talking about and build trust

Never ask for the money!

Never ask for the money, especially on the first meeting. I host a couple of networking events and you see people all the time trying to raise money and sell their business plan or idea to a total stranger during a two-minute conversation. It comes across as very unprofessional and puts people off immediately. Start by getting their contact details and then getting to know them – aim to gain credibility and look to understand what it is they want or need from the partnership. Find out what the most important thing to them is; it's not about you, it's about THEM! Always under-promise and over-deliver; there's nothing worse than over-promising and setting unachievable expectations. When starting out, you might feel that you need to big up the deal to get the investment, but trust me, it will come back to bite you later when you have an unhappy JV partner to deal with.

The most important factors in someone's decision to joint venture with you or not will usually be any one or more of the following:

- Trust

- Credibility

- Likeability

- Reliability

- Focus

- Drive

Trust:

Do you come across as a trustworthy person and do they?

Credibility:

Do you come across as credible and are your deals credible? Do you know what you're talking about? Have you got a good knowledge of your area and what types of returns you can get from different properties? Can you talk about different investment strategies that can be used to make you and your JV partner more money?

Likeability:

For some people it won't matter how good a deal is if they don't like the other party. Different people are attracted to different things; this is great news, as there will always be people who are attracted to you and people who are not – that's life! You don't need to work with everyone, but just knowing that some people will like you and what you're trying to achieve is a real confidence booster and proves that knowledge and experience are not always most important things, often likeability is the key factor in a person's decision making.

Reliability:

Can you be relied upon to deliver what you promise? Have you got a track record of reliability? This does not have to be in property, you can demonstrate other areas of your life where you have been reliable to give your JV partner confidence.

Focussed:

Are you focussed or are you someone who keeps jumping from one idea to another without ever finishing anything? FOCUS stands for Follow One Course Until Successful.

Drive:

Are you driven to succeed? How much do you want the success? What are you willing to do to achieve the results? How ambitious are you?

Did you notice that none of those six factors mentioned a requirement to already have property? If you are starting out, you have many skills that a more experienced investor or wealthy person needs to continue to grow. If you can demonstrate some or all of the above traits you won't ever need to ask for the money, people will start to offer it to you. The most important thing is that you need to believe in yourself, back yourself and never give up on your dreams.

Exercise: How investible are you? Before you read on, get a pen and a blank piece of paper and take a few minutes to list all the current skills you have. I'll get you started: things like knowledge of certain strategies, knowledge of your area, being friends with a local estate agent, skills from your job that are beneficial in property, access to a successful property investor who can advise and mentor you, time to dedicate to the business, etc. Ok over to you, make that list!

Now make a list of all the things you need that are currently not on your list, and then start to plan to either learn them, outsource them or JV with someone who has that missing thing that you need to make you a success.

Different ways to structure a JV

There are several different ways to structure a JV partnership depending on what it is you and your prospective JV partner want – for example, are you keeping the properties long term or are you looking to secure a deal, refurbish and sell, etc.? There are so many variables and the best way to start is to sit down with your prospective JV partner and each list all the things that are most important to you. Then you can structure the JV agreement in the best way to suit each of your needs.

The most common JV structures are as follows:

- **Mortgage host / deed of trust (DoT)**

  This is where one party agrees to take out a mortgage on a property in their name and the other person has a deed of trust (also known as a declaration of trust). A deed of trust is a legal document that states 'trustees' are appointed to hold property for 'beneficiaries'. It appoints people as trustees who are 'trusted' to act in an appropriate manner and always in the interests of the beneficiaries and is governed by The Trustee Act 2000. In this case, the trustee would be the mortgage host and the beneficiary would be the JV partner who doesn't host the mortgage. The DoT will state what share of equity and cash flow the beneficiary is entitled to from the deal. These are great when two people don't want to be linked on a credit file.

- **50-50 JV**

  This is where two parties agree to an equal 50-50 share of any upside or downside in a deal. They may or may not put in an equal amount of time and money. The 50-50 agreement can be structured based on the equity and cash flow split after each party has been paid back their initial investment of cash or paid for their time input.

- **One for you, one for me JV**

  This is where parties agree to buy properties but don't want to be financially linked to each other, so they structure a partnership where the first deal is purchased in the name of one partner, the second in the name of the other partner and so on, so every second deal becomes yours. You can structure this with a JV partner so you find the deals and they put the cash in on a buy-refurbish-refinance model, and the party putting the money in gets the first deal. After the property is refinanced and the initial setup money has been taken back out, the money is then used to buy a second property in your name, and this continues one for you, one for me.

- **Time for money**

  This is where one person puts their time into a partnership in exchange for the other person's money and can be used in conjunction with any of the structures we have just discussed.

- **Knowledge for money**

  This is where one person brings their knowledge to the partnership and the other person puts the money in. In this arrangement, both partners put time into the partnership; what each person's time is spent on is agreed at the start.

- **Less cash flow for more equity**

  It can be common in a joint venture that one person is more interested in the equity than the cash flow or vice versa. When I started out in property, the one thing I needed the most was monthly cash flow to get me out of my job; you can't spend equity, so although it's great to have for the future, it was not going to replace my monthly salary.

Now that I've built up a sizable property portfolio with much more monthly positive cash flow than I need or want to spend, cash flow is now not as important as it once was. Equity is now of greater interest to me as it can sit in the property and allow me to build a long-term legacy. You will also have a preference today in terms of what is most important to you but try not to push this onto the other person – focus on what is most important to them, solve their need and you will make a lot of cash.

Any one of the joint venture partnerships I have just described can be done either in your personal name or by setting up a limited company, depending on the reason for the partnership and each party's current tax position. It is always best to speak to a specialist property tax advisor before entering into any type of JV partnership.

Case study: Former public house conversion to 8-bed HMO

I held an 'investors' day' in my investment area, to which I invited some people who I met at a property event for the day to have a look at the town and see some of the deals we were working on. Hosting investor days is a great way to qualify people you meet at events, because if they are willing to get on the train or in their car and come to your area, then they are serious about investing. In my early days as an investor, I used to worry about inviting other investors to my area, as I thought it might just create competition. There is a risk that this could happen, but if you don't do it, you won't get as many JV partners to invest in you, which means you can't buy the properties anyway. There are always a few people who will try and take advantage of you for a day to learn about the area, but they will still never be able to compete with you long-term as they are not on the ground every day in the area and will never know the area as well as you – you know the good streets, the bad streets and so on, and you can't learn that level of detail in a day.

So back to the deal. At the end of the investor day, a couple approached me and said they had money to invest and would be interested in working with me. We agreed to have a one-to-one meeting and we sat down and discussed what each party wanted and our long-term goals. Both of us wanted to hold property long-term and they had a target of doing one deal per month for 36 months. The quantity of deals was sufficient for me to agree to set up a limited company on a 50-50 JV agreement in which I would source the deals, manage the refurbishments and manage the tenants long-term via our in-house letting agency and they would put the funds in. All invested funds would get paid back to them before I made any profit, but from the point at which they had all their funds back out, we would split equity and cash flow 50-50. Now they wanted one property a month for 36 months, but you should never over-promise and under-deliver, so I told them upfront that I felt this was not achievable. I explained there were outside factors not under my control, such as how long refurbishments would take on different properties and how long the refinancing process would take once the refurbishments were completed on each deal.

I have now purchased four properties with them, all using none of my own money, and this former public house is one of the deals. It was a property I had been driving past on a regular basis but it didn't really catch my eye as it looked too small. But then one afternoon when I was visiting the estate agency on our high street, one of the agents told me I needed to view the property, as it was bigger than it look and had a lot of potential, so I agreed to have a look.

The building had been purchased by a couple a few years earlier and they had applied for planning permission and change of use to convert it from a pub into a 3-bed family home. Once the planning permission was approved they started the conversion works and ran into some difficulties, which led to friction in the relationship that resulted in them separating, so they placed the property on the market for sale. When we purchased the building, it was part refurbished but was still a blank canvas, able to be converted to an HMO. We agreed a purchase price of £135,000 and applied for change of use from a residential home to an HMO. In my experience, I knew it would be difficult to get a change of use from public house to HMO, but it was easier to get one from a dwelling house to an HMO – the couple had helped us with our application by already having an initial change of use and having started the works.

The numbers

- Purchase price: £135,000

- Refurbishment costs (including purchase fees): £45,000 (note: most of the works were complete)

- Total costs: £180,000

- Revaluation as an 8-bed HMO: £230,000

- Mortgage at 75% LTV: £174,800 at 5.49% = £799.71 pcm

- Total monthly costs after refinancing (pcm): £799.71 mortgage + £550 bills = £1,349.71

- Rental income (pcm): £3,033

- Profit (pcm): £1.683.29 (£841.64 each)

Just one deal, giving me an £841.64 profit per month plus a 50% share of the equity in a property that I put none of my own funds into. How many of these do you need to do to change your life? How many can you do? AS MANY AS YOU CAN FIND WHEN YOU ARE YOUR OWN LOTTERY

Case Study: Steve Bridson – private money lending

The following are Steve's words:

I attended some property training with Kevin to learn about specialist property strategies and to meet individuals who were actively looking to source and secure investments that I could potentially lend money on. As a private money lender, I wanted to ensure I understood the strategies I was lending my money for, but I also wanted to ensure I knew that the people I was lending to had the right knowledge.

At one of these property events I met a man who had set up a Rent2Rent business in the London area; we got chatting and I told him I was interested in doing R2R. He told me that his goal was to manage 500 properties using the R2R model then sell the business for an 8-figure sum. I was very impressed with the business model and wanted to know more.

I had several meetings with him and eventually agreed to invest £30,000 with the company to help them set up three or four properties – the figure was quite high as the refurbs were of a very high standard. All the deals were done on a minimum of a five-year contract. At this time, he only had around 10-15 properties. As I was one of the first to invest, I had a very good return on my investment. I subsequently went on to invest another £20,000 in the business.

Whilst talking to friends and work colleagues about what I had done, some of them were very interested as the returns they could receive for lending their money were substantially more than they were getting at the bank. I had a discussion with the company director and discussed whether I could receive commission for finding people with money to invest in his company; we agreed that he would pay me 1% commission on any money I could secure. I recommended a few friends and business colleagues who had money to invest and I started getting 1% for the amount lent, so if they lent £10K I would receive £100 fixed for 36 months, which is the duration of the loan.

I now regularly go to property meetings and find new clients with money to lend just by telling people what I do, and a lot of my clients have invested several times now. To date I have done 19 deals, and it's increasing month on month.

You do the work once, they say – that's the case for me, and I get paid for three years. I started out wanting to learn about creative property strategies so I could invest my own money, but now thanks to learning from Kevin, I make my money from investing other people's money – truly No Money Down.

Case study: Ruth and Gillian Hobbs – Commercial Conversions

The following are Gillian's words:

We've been working together on residential flips and BTLs in London in our own names, but in January 2018 we formalised our working relationship with a limited company – Urban Sister Developments. We will be focussed on replacing our income forever using the money we've created through property to buy and hold; although we had created cash, we had no monthly passive income. We thought we could do this initially using the cash we had created to buy and hold one big commercial to residential deal.

There is immense competition for office to residential schemes that are outside article 4 areas, as these would generally fall under prior approval schemes (with some exceptions), and therefore not need planning to convert. We found it incredibly difficult to locate these schemes as they have become so popular – you need to be 'in' with the agent and know what you are talking about, especially as first-time commercial developers.

However, after a quick change of tack we started looking at long-term office buildings within our golden triangle that were for rent, not for sale. This may sound a bit strange, but we figured we could offer an option to purchase on a lease, or we could simply offer to purchase outright, on the basis the vendor could not find a let. My first call yielded a success – we hit gold by phoning up about this current building, Majority House, which we have renamed The Lofts. [As the image and branding are part of our strategy, the name needs to resonate with our target market.] The building was up for rent for three years without success and the vendor decided to sell that day we phoned.

We saw the building within two hours of speaking to the agent, we put our cards on the table immediately and told him we were serious and wanted to put in an offer – we didn't want anyone else to see it, we didn't want to enter a bidding war. Our exact words were: "What do you want me to offer to get this off the market today? I don't want anyone else to see it." The words were important because this immediately put him in the driving seat, and I did exactly what he told me – put in a full price offer.

We didn't negotiate on the price the vendor wanted, as it was already a reasonable price given what we wanted to achieve with the building; my gut feeling was it could have been priced higher. We also knew that other developers were being called as we were being shown round. Gillian worked on the financials within those critical two hours, and with our vision of luxury student accommodation, we were able to show this was more than a viable project.

The deal was funded wholly in cash by flipping properties in London with a two-year hold. We found that by buying run-down 1-bed properties, we could convert to 2-beds, rent out for two years and then sell, making at least 40% margins; in some cases, we made 150% due to the increase in the property market. We had achieved over asking on our final bigger project, which was sold for £1.26M (purchased for £615K) via sealed bids in a stagnant London market. Each property we have flipped sticks to a strict finished look and feel in line with our branding and core values. Staging properties is at the heart of our strategy, giving the buyer the dream of what they didn't know they wanted. The pipeline kept flipping over until eventually we've made enough to purchase The Lofts in cash, with spare cash to purchase our second commercial conversion.

The Lofts is located in the heart of the student village area in Derby. We have received full approval for change of use from commercial to residential (use class C3), then converting over to four 6-bed flats with six students, totalling 24 students, all with en-suites (use class C4). This is a hold strategy for long-term income which will replace our income in almost one deal. The intention is to utilise a commercial mortgage that will take into consideration our projected gross rental yield of around £140K in order to get back out all of our initial investment, thereby making the deal, which will be valued at over £1.1M, a 'no money left in' deal!

Our property portfolio started with a £40K loan from family, and now between us we are up to a GDV of £6.5M with most of the growth happening in the last year. Our strategy is fundamentally based around the principles of No Money Down Investing, something we would never have known had we not been educated on how to build a property portfolio starting from nothing.

The next projects we are looking at are all using other people's money. We have an offer in on a large building in Ealing, but this will be funded by high net worth investors who, through the power of networking and social media, have approached us to invest. We have not had to ask investors to buy into our deals, if you do the numbers and they support a project, and you have the guts to go for it, investors come to you – that's a valuable lesson we have learnt.

Success like this by ordinary people is the reason why I'm so keen to get this knowledge out to the masses – I believe that with the right education everyone can build a similar business, no matter what their starting point. One of the main reasons people never get started is because they believe they need money to create money; you don't! Money is not power, knowledge is power. You need knowledge to start the flow of money towards you, the money is all around us! When you learn the principles of No Money Down Investing, the limit to how many deals you do is simply down to your goals and aspirations and not your bank balance!

Chapter 14 – How to Use the Law of Adverse Possession to Your Advantage

There is a lot of talk in property communities about adverse possession, what it is and how you can use it to get property for free. What I have learnt over the years is that the thing about talk is that it's just that... Talk.

In this chapter I am going to explain to you what adverse possession means, the legalities around it and what you can and cannot do. I believe it's a very powerful tool to help you with your property journey, but it is not something that you can actually use to take control of someone else's property. Even if it was, I wouldn't use the adverse possession process to do this, because apart from all the legal complications, I believe it's also just fundamentally unethical. Sorry to burst your bubble before we even get into the detail, but please stick with me as this is something that can really help you find great deals.

So, what is adverse possession? It is a doctrine under which a person can claim the legal rights to a property that is unoccupied, run down or derelict, or where the owner cannot be contacted, such as when the last remaining heir to the property has passed away – this includes houses and land.

How did the law come about?

If you look back through history, it is littered with examples of statutes allowing people to claim or gain title to land through adverse possession. The concept of adverse possession first appeared in a portion of the Code of Hammurabi, some 2000 years BC. Law 30 of the code states: "If a chieftain or a man leaves his house, garden, and field and someone else takes possession of his house, garden, and field and uses it for three years: if the first owner return and claims his house, garden, and field, it shall not be given to him, but he who has taken possession of it and used it shall continue to use it".

However, there are some exceptions to this rule listed in the Code of Hammurabi; the exceptions where the land can be reclaimed are as follows:

- For a soldier captured in battle

- A soldier killed in battle

- If the landowner had a juvenile son and he returned to stake a claim when he became an adult

Fast-forward to today and what the current law states: to claim a title, certain common law requirements need to be met, and the person claiming adverse possession needs to be able to prove that they have been in possession for a sufficient period of time, as defined by the statute of limitations. The common law requirements have regularly changed over time and can vary depending on your location. However, in most cases, for an adverse possessor to obtain title, his possession of the property must be:

- Continuous – this means that the person claiming possession must maintain continuous possession of the property. However, the continuity may be maintained between successive adverse possessors if there is privity between them.

- Hostile – this means that the possession infringes on the rights of the true owner. If the true owner consents or gives licence to the adverse possessor's use of the property, possession is not hostile and it is not really adverse possession, e.g. if you are just renting a property from a landlord then you cannot stake a claim to the title of that property under adverse possession, no matter how long you have occupied the property.

- Open and notorious – this means that the possession of the property must be obvious to anyone who bothers to look so that they have the opportunity to inform the true owner of the adverse possession should the true owner be known to them. It's this part of the law that we can use to help find great property deals; I will discuss this in detail later.

- Actual – the adverse possessor is actually in possession of someone else's property. The true owner has a cause of action for trespass, which must be pursued within the statute of limitations.

- Exclusive – the adverse possessor does not share control of the property with anyone else (unless in privity with himself). He excludes others from possession, as if he was actual owner.

So, that means adverse possession requires factual possession of the land or property, with the intention to possess without the owner's consent, and must use the land or property in the manner in which it is meant to be used – i.e. if it is a house it must be used as a home to live in or rented out and be taken care of like a home should be, it cannot be left empty. If it is a piece of land it must be used in the way it is meant to be used, such as lawns taken care of or vegetables or trees planted and maintained, etc.

Source: Cornell Law School
Link: https://www.law.cornell.edu/wex/adverse_possession

How long does the adverse possession process take?

You must prove that the squatter and any predecessors through whom they claim have been in adverse possession for at least 10 years for claims completed after 13 October 2003 (prior to this it was 12 years). You cannot apply for the title until the 10 years have elapsed and you must be able to prove the 10-year possession; once the 10 years have passed you can then apply for possession and give the landowner a statutory period of time (65 business days) to object to the adverse possession, and if they do so, the application fails unless:

(Now for some legal jargon…)

1. It would be unconscionable because of an equity by estoppel for the registered proprietor to seek to dispossess the squatter and the squatter ought in the circumstances to be registered as proprietor, or

2. The squatter is for some other reason entitled to be registered as proprietor, or

3. The squatter has been in adverse possession of land adjacent to their own under the mistaken but reasonable belief that they are the owner of it, the exact line of the boundary with this adjacent land has not been determined and the estate to which the application relates was registered more than a year prior to the date of the application.

Note that where adverse possession is claimed in respect of land owned by a company which has been dissolved and there has been disclaimer by the Crown or Royal Duchy so that escheat has taken place, an application based on adverse possession cannot be made under Schedule 6: the registered estate will have determined.

Source: gov.uk
Link: https://www.gov.uk/government/publications/adverse-possession-of-registered-land/practice-guide-4-adverse-possession-of-registered-land

A few famous examples of adverse possession

The case of Harry Hallowes is one of the UK's most famous adverse possession cases in the recent past. In 2008, Harry acquired title to a plot of garden land in London worth an estimated £4M at the time by camping on it for 21 years. Although this is an extreme case in terms of the value of the property acquired, there are lots of people who 'acquire' unused lands next to their gardens and houses – this is often done by planting the area or including it as part of their cared for garden area and then in time moving their boundary fence to include the unused land within their garden fence boundary.

There is a neighbour of mine in Ireland who had a field on either side of this old grass walkthrough that had been used in the past but was being used less and less as time passed by. When I was a just a kid, he knocked down the walls on either side of the walkthrough and included the public walkthrough as part of his field, combining the two fields into one. He has now used this land for over 20 years and it has never been questioned.

Another example is that of Jack Blackburn. Jack was a struggling artist who became the owner of the £100,000 council flat he had squatted in for 13 years. Jack had always regarded the second floor 1-bedroom property in Brixton, South London as his home, and after three years of squatting, he secured official ownership when judges ruled he had the right to keep it.

Source: Daily Mail
Link http://www.dailymail.co.uk/news/article-53579/Squatter-owner-100-000-flat.html

An elderly couple who had cut a wealthy neighbour's grass verge for 12 years were given the land in another 'squatters' rights' ruling. Property consultant Marcus Heaney got embroiled in a lengthy court battle with pensioners Hilary and Edward Kirkby over the patch of grass in Thorp Arch, near Wetherby, West Yorkshire and eventually the couple won the case and were given legal rights to the grass verge.

Source: The Telegraph
Link: https://www.telegraph.co.uk/news/2016/05/25/couple-who-cut-wealthy-neighbours-grass-verge-for-12-years-given/

How can you prove possession?

I hear a lot of people say that you can fast-track the process by putting a sign on a property stating that you are claiming it under the law of adverse possession and take a picture of yourself outside of the property with a newspaper to show the date of the possession – and that you could use an old newspaper to get past the 10 year requirement. This is simply not true. What is true is that you could use a newspaper to show the date you put a sign up, but you need to comply with all the requirements of the law to be successful in a claim, therefore you need to prove continuous, hostile, open and notorious, actual and exclusive use of the property to be able to successfully claim. This is where you run into problems – in order to make a successful claim, you need to do something illegal, which is break into a property that is not yours!

What you need to do for a successful claim is look for:

1. Empty properties

2. Boarded up properties

3. Overgrown gardens

4. Overgrown land

Once you identify a potential property, you should then mitigate the risk of a returning owner – you don't want to spend time and money on someone else's property only for them to return and take the property back. You can mitigate the risk by:

1. Writing a letter to the property or leaflet drop the property – this is the starting point before you do anything else, as surprisingly, houses that look empty are often occupied.

2. Do a Land Registry check to see who the listed owner is or if the property is unlisted.

3. Speak to neighbours and see if they have any information about the previous occupiers – maybe they have a contact number or know where the owners or their relatives are.

4. Hire a tracing agent – they can check old library records, hospital records, death notices, etc. to identify if there are any living relatives that could stake a claim to the property.

Let's say you have done all of the above and it has resulted in no evidence of a living person with a claim to the property. The next steps would be to start to take control and begin to show proof of you taking care of the property.

Step 1: Put a sign on the property stating that under the law of adverse possession you are taking control of the property as of said date, and should anyone have any objections to this they should contact you on xxx number.

Step 2: Take photos on day you took control; you can use a newspaper to show the date, but you also want to show pictures of the property condition to prove you have maintained and improved it.

Step 3: Keep receipts for any money spent on refurbishment to show you have improved the property.

Step 4: Keep proof of payment of bills for council tax, gas, electric, water, etc. – this is much more effective than a picture of a newspaper!

Step 5: Carry out ongoing maintenance and take regular pictures.

Here is where the claim falls down and why I don't do adverse possession – and why I suggest you don't either. In order to carry out maintenance on a property, you must break into the property and this in itself is an illegal act! There are many perfectly legal ways to become seriously wealthy from property investing, many of which we have covered in earlier chapters of this book, so there is no need to do anything illegal. And even if it was not illegal, it would still be unethical. However, keep reading, as there is one part of the adverse possession process that I do recommend you do, which is not illegal or unethical and that can be the starting point to making you a lot of money.

Before we cover this part of the process, I think it's important to share that I do know some people who have taken control of properties with the intention of claiming them in the future under the law of adverse possession, but I don't personally know anyone who has made a successful claim.

On a couple of claims I'm aware of, the following has happened:

Investor 1 – let's call him Joe. Joe had taken possession of a property in East London, refurbished it and rented it out by the room as a multi let. Joe employed the services of a local letting agent to manage the property and everything was fine for several months. Joe's plan was to make enough profit from the rental income to get back his initial investment and then, if he never managed to claim legal title in the future, he wouldn't be out of pocket financially. On the face of it, this was a good plan, not knowing anyone who has actually managed to be successful in a claim for title. However, Joe became friendly with the letting agents and one day decided to tell them how smart he had been in taking possession of the property. A few weeks passed and on the date the rents were usually received from the letting agency, nothing arrived. He rang the agents and was told the boss wasn't available. Days turned into a couple of weeks and he was still getting no reply from the agents. Joe went to the agency and confronted the agent face to face – the agent told him that he would be keeping the rent and if he had any problems with that he could take him to court. The agent knew that it was impossible for Joe to take him to court, as he was not the legal owner of the property and therefore had no legal right to the rental income.

Investor 2 – let's call her Sue. Sue had taken possession of a property, refurbished it and let it out by the room as a multi let. A few months passed by and Sue began to get friendly with one of the tenants; she began to see the tenant as more of a friend than a tenant and of course, you tell your friends everything, right? Well one day Sue let slip to her tenant friend that she did not own the house but that she had in fact taken control of it and was going to use the law of adverse possession to apply for absolute title in the future. Within a few days, Sue got a message from the tenant saying that they'd had a think about what she told them and not only were they no longer going to pay the rent but they also wanted to be paid to keep their mouth shut and not tell the other tenants about how Sue had acquired the property – a very expensive lesson indeed for Sue!

So, can you take control of an empty property, refurbish it and live in it or rent it out? In a word, yes! Is it legal to do so? NO!

If you did break the law and gain entry to another person's house and get away with it, would you be able to claim legal title after 10 years? Possibly, but I'm not aware of any successful cases relating to property investors, and it is not something that I would do or support due to illegalities and ethics of it.

So what would I do?

As discussed in earlier chapters, a lot of my property purchases are done direct to vendor (D2V) and from experience of doing deals via estate agents and D2V, I believe you will more often than not be able to negotiate a better deal D2V. We've discussed the best strategies for going D2V in chapter 6: Marketing. Let's say you've seen a potentially empty and run down property where there is clearly room to add value through refurbishment, and it's in the area of town where you are investing. You've tried leaflet dropping and posting a letter but had no reply; you then tried a Land Registry search and speaking to the neighbours, but you've been told it has been empty for a long time and nobody has any details on the owners. In a scenario like this, Step 1 of adverse possession, discussed earlier in this chapter, is a brilliant way of "fishing out" the owners and getting them to ring you: putting a sign on the property stating that you are taking control of the property as of xxx date under the law of adverse possession and should anyone have any objections to this they should contact you on xxx number. If the owners exist, or if anyone has any contact details for them, I guarantee you once you put a sign on their property they will be in touch with you quickly.

Now be prepared, because when they ring you they won't be very happy. What you need to do is make sure you don't put your personal number on the sign – get a 'burn phone', which is basically just a pay as you go SIM card in an old phone, and wait for it to ring. You know when it rings that it can only be ringing in relation to your sign on the property, so when it rings, whatever you do, DON'T ANSWER IT! This will be the point at which the owner is at their angriest, so it won't be a good time to discuss their property with them. You want to leave it for a few hours until they have calmed down a little and then ring them back. Start by apologising and explaining that you had no intention of taking ownership of their property; explain that you are a local property problem solver and had seen the house was empty, had tried everything you could think of to contact them to see what their plans were for the property. Then you remembered that you once read a book by this crazy Irish guy who said that if you put a sign on the property, the owners would definitely be in touch.

Now that you have them on the phone, you can ask them what are their plans are for the property. Would they be interested in selling? Maybe they want to refurbish the house but don't have the money – a possible assisted sale, vendor finance, Rent2Rent, BMV purchase or lease option opportunity can be agreed and everyone is a winner.

This is a really powerful method of getting D2V for property deals where you don't have to do anything illegal; there are lots of examples within the property communities of people who use these signs very successfully to fish out homeowners. One example is Lee Northrop from Stockport, who followed the steps I've discussed in this chapter and had a successful outcome, as shown below.

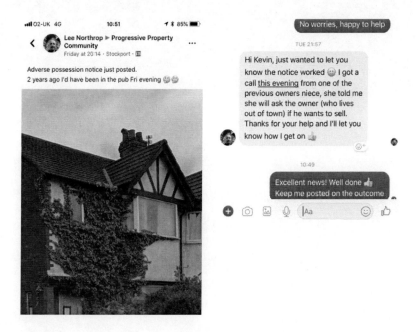

Chapter 15: Next Steps

How many deals do you want? And more importantly, why? Jim Rohn once famously spoke about having a dollar and some ambition, and this is so true – the biggest mistake you can do is to do nothing! You have learnt strategies in this book that can change your life beyond what you ever thought possible; you have learnt strategies that most people will never get to learn. Most people never get the opportunity to take their financial future into their own hands. This book gives you that opportunity – all you need is a pound and some ambition! The question is what are you going to do now?

Are you going to take the next step to your financial freedom? Are you going to implement what you have learnt? Are you going to expand on your education? We are all learning all the time and will never know everything, that's why the power is in your network – you become what you think about most of the time! Spend time with successful people, learn from successful people and you will become successful.

No matter what your starting point, you can be successful.

I started with £135K of debt – that sounds like a lot of money, and it is a lot of money if you are trying to save it in a job. However, the reality is it's not difficult to get out of that sort of debt using the strategies you have learnt in this book. Making money is not difficult, what's difficult is not being able to do the things you want to do in life, not being able to provide for your family, your kids, your parents, your grandparents, whatever it may be. Not being able to do the things that are important to you in life is difficult.

Focus on replacing your income first to get out of your job, then focus on getting to financial comfort where you feel you can spend money on what you want, when you want. Once you are at this point, you can focus on creating enough assets and passive income to leave a legacy for your family for generations to come. No Money Down Investing is the way to get there – and get there quickly.

I will leave you with my top four tips for creating a legacy level income:

- Focus on achieving positive monthly cash flow – don't focus on capital growth, focus on rental income. Cash flow is king.

- Have a long-term vision – long term, house prices will automatically increase in value, giving you capital growth. However, you need to buy and control properties for cash flow today, you can't spend equity, but you can spend cash flow.

- If you need money for a deal, use other people's money. I've been in property since 2004, and I've seen so many companies go bust in a recession. The reason most companies with small or big portfolios go bust is because they focused on buying assets and capital growth, and they totally forgot about cash flow. You have got to have cash in the bank. You've got to have cash! This is why you need to do No Money Down Investing, because if you've got money right now and you put it all into property, what happens when the rainy day comes? What happens if interest rates go up? What happens if three or four boilers need replacing at the same time and you don't have the money to pay for it? What happens if you get hit with a big repair bill? The smart investors use other people's money or no money. Use the vendor's money, use tenant buyers' money, use joint venture partners money, use private investors' funds and keep your own cash liquid. Whenever anything happens, then you've got a big enough cash buffer to survive in any market condition. The reason companies go into liquidation is because they don't have any cash in the bank; they expand too quickly. You're a business now. You've got to make sure you've got cash flow and cash in the bank.

- Get the help of a coach or a mentor — I tried to do property on my own for over 10 years and found more failures than successes. I then invested in my education and aligned myself to successful investors who had walked the road before me, and it completely changed my life in just a couple of years. I will continue to have mentors for the rest of my life. You've invested in this book, and hopefully you've found it to be a valuable investment. You see, you don't know what you don't know, and we all miss out on opportunities in life, not from a lack of money but from a lack of knowledge! You have got to commit to continuing to expand your knowledge and be held accountable to implementing that new knowledge. Reading a book doesn't make you successful, action makes you successful, and you need a mentor to hold you accountable. There is not a successful person in any walk of life who was not coached and mentored in some way towards that success.

Glossary of terms

AST – Assured Shorthold Tenancy	LTV – Loan to Value
AP – Adverse Possession	NMD – No Money Down
AV – Adding Value	OPM – Other People's Money
B2F – Buy2Flip	PA – Per Annum
B2L – Buy2Let	pcm – Per Calendar Month
BMV – Below Market Value	POA – Power of Attorney
D2V – Direct to Vendor	PG – Planning Gain
EDC – Exchange with Delayed Completion	R2B – Rent2Buy
EPC – Energy Performance Certificate	R2O – Rent2Own
ERC – Early Redemption Charge	R2R – Rent2Rent
FTB – First-Time Buyer	ROCE – Return on Capital Employed
GDPR – General data protection regulation	ROI – Return on Investment
GDV – Gross Development Value	SA – Serviced Accommodation
HMO – House of Multiple Occupation	SARB – Sale and Rent Back
HoT – Head of Terms	SVR – Standard Variable Rate
IO – Interest Only	TS – Title Split
JV – Joint Venture	VF – Vendor Finance
LO – Lease Option	